Space-Time-Consciousness

Edited by: **Gopa Guha**

About the Authors

Dr. Bhaskar Vyas (1937) is a plastic surgeon and a retired professor of the Medical College, Vadodara. He has also been a member of faculty at the Psychology Department, The M.S. University. Consciousness has been a prime interest for his research. This has led him to be a perennial student of philosophy. Presently he is conducting stem cell research focused on regeneration and rejuvenation.

Dr. Rajni Vyas (1937) is an obstetrician and gynaecologist. She has been a professor at The M.S. University, Vadodra.

Apart from her own discipline, she has taught psychology and hypnotherapy as well. Her seminal research contribution is in the field of infertility of unknown origin. She has conducted stem cell research with significant contribution in diabetes and osteoarthritis. This husband-wife research association has produced over 30 publications each. They have taught hypnotherapy all across India as well as at international conferences. Their other publications are on holistic health, Raj Yoga, philosophy of justice, and on cultural topics. They have also been biographers of the Dalai Lama.

Space-Time-Consciousness

Rationale of Paranormal

Bhaskar Vyas
Rajni Vyas

CONCEPT PUBLISHING COMPANY PVT. LTD.
NEW DELHI-110059

ISBN-13: 978-93-5439-052-4

First Published 2021

Published and Printed by

Since 1974

Concept Publishing Company Pvt. Ltd.
Regd. Office:
A/15-16, Commercial Block, Mohan Garden,
New Delhi-110059 (INDIA)
Phones : 25351460, 25351794, *Fax* : 091-11-25357109
E-mail : publishing@conceptpub.com
Website: www.conceptpub.com

Cataloging in Publication Data--Courtesy: D.K. Agencies (P) Ltd. <docinfo@dkagencies.com>

Vyas, Bhaskar, author.
Space-time-consciousness : rationale of the paranormal / Bhaskar Vyas, Rajni Vyas.
pages cm
Contributed articles.
Includes bibliographical references and index.
ISBN 9789354390524

1. Space and time. 2. Consciousness. 3. Logical positivism. 4. Science—Philosophy. 5. Buddhist philosophy. 6. Cosmology. I. Vyas, Rajni, author. II. Title.

LCC BD632.V93 2021 | DDC 115 23

Preface

In the autumn of year 2001, we met His Holiness the Dalai Lama at Dharamsala. We presented him our recently published book, *The Collision of Culture* and discussed our plans to write a biographical work, *Experiments with the Truth and Non-violence*. We also asked him about his ongoing discussion with the Western philosophers and scientists. Mr. Tenzin Geyche, his personal secretary then presented us with the entire series of dialogues published as books. The books mainly covered space, time and consciousness. Browsing through the books, it appeared that 'East is East and West is West; and never the twain shall meet.' The scientific domain and western philosophy appeared to be remotely distant from the esoteric concepts of mind and consciousness in Tibetan Buddhism.

On second reflection, we wondered, was it really so? Gautama Buddha advised to follow the path of reason. Certainly then, Buddhist precepts would yield to logic and logical positivism. Philosophy is the mother of all sciences. Since the philosophers do not wait for the empirical proofs, may be their vision jumps centuries or millennia. We realized that in the meditative way of Mahayana and Vajrayana traditions as well as in the Raj-yoga of Patanjali, there is a way to get an intuitive glimpse of reconciliation.

Prof. Jayant Narlikar gave introduction of Prof. George Sudershan and Prof. Raja Ramanna to Prof. B.V. Srikantan who spared time for personal discussions on several occasions. Dr. Sudhir Shah and Vasantbhai Patel discussed paranormal occurrences and corresponded too. Kirti Vijay Maharaj sat for many hours with us to browse through many Jain texts. Ms. Jyoti Mukerji volunteered for age regression. Ashwin Mehta provided the photograph of a galaxy from the laboratory of Prof. Jayant Narlikar (IUCAA) that adorns the cover page. Ernest and Kathryn

Rossi permitted us to use the photograph in Fig. 4. For all these and many more, we are grateful.

The use of perfect language is indeed a task of high complexity. This is particularly so with physics. A small correction of a word or grammar can so change the syntax that the meaning may entirely differ. Or the subjective semantic interpretation may cause two differently meaning statements look alike. For errors, of this kind, if any we take the entire responsibility.

We also wish to note our appreciation for the publishers, Mr. Ashok Mittal and Mr. Nitin Mittal.

Contents

List of Tables and Figures

LIST OF TABLES

LIST OF FIGURES

1
Introduction

This presentation examines the concepts of space, time and consciousness through Modern Scientific Mode. The modalities under exploration are, at the first look, taken for granted. It needs just a little reflection to realize that space is taken for granted as an area defined by boundaries; our understanding of time is that it is an interval between two events; and consciousness is hardly reflected upon. Of course, our world exists because we are conscious of it. All the three modalities need to be explored in depth when we wish to understand them through questions that the science usually asks like, what, why, how, when and such probes.

Philosophical traditions like Buddhist tradition as well as postulates of Patanjali in Classical Indian tradition*, grapple with them. Though based on reason, they rely heavily on inductive logic. Inductive logic is a sound tool with limitation that even one exception will falsify the hypothesis. Therefore, since the rise of Age of Reason, science has provided answers with such certainty that the results may be falsified by the same means—empirical scientific data.

The thesis postulates a concept of additional Fifth Dimension† to the universe, as "space-time-consciousness". At the onset there is an attempt to understand space, time and space-time‡ through the empirical data as it obtains in the discipline of physics. It then explores altered states of consciousness—meditation and alike—

* Patanjali (about 2500 B.C.) has described an elaborate system of yoga, known as Raj-yoga.

† Dimension is a product of basic physical qualities.

‡ In Newtonian physics, space is considered as composed of three mutually perpendicular dimensions. Time is a separate entity. In Einsteinian physics, space and time are combined into a four-dimensional continuum that is termed as space-time (*vide infra*).

as a gateway to the fifth dimension. The approach is from the phenomenal to the spiritual. The validation is from the empirical and experiential data as well as epistemological concepts of Buddhist Philosophy and Classical Indian Philosophy.

The scientific revelations of last century have been spectacular. In each and every discipline of science, there is enormous generation of new data, leading to vast expansion of understanding. Thus, our knowledge of the natural laws that govern the universe has made quantum strides. The mysteries of life have been unveiled: the life is synthesized in a test tube. We are now face to face with fundamental stuff of life since we have mapped out the genetic code. Cloning has happened: raising questions of enormous magnitude as to what exactly a being is. Let us leave aside the ethereal questions like the souls of the clones so that we have not to prove that the souls of the clones are separate or bonded. The clone is derived from the same stuff as the parent clone. Then, do we have an answer to the question: what will happen to the self of the remaining clone when the other one dies? If we were to accept only a materialistic explanation that "me is what I call myself" and there was nothing except the play of physics and biochemistry in the form of physicality of being, it will still leave such a question unanswered.

Design, Purpose and God

And the question whether there is some design or purpose or "something" else that is intangible and yet governing the universe is still to be answered: probably it never will be answered. The functioning of all the living systems is so construed as to constantly protect themselves. We may be able to decipher the physical laws that govern the behaviour of the animals so that it is possible to explain such phenomena like the migration of the birds and psychosis of the schizophrenics. However, be it at the gigantic cosmological scale or at the molecular biological measure like the behaviour of a white blood corpuscle, a teleological* purpose that keeps the system functional does seem to be lurking behind such

---

* Teleological purpose cannot be said to be a scientific proposition. The behaviour that aids survival is scientifically explained by the anthropic principles (*vide infra*). Yet, its usage is deliberate here since it reflects authors' hunch.

events, even if they were to be explained on the natural principles. Assumptive as it seems, it appears almost absurd to deny the operation of intangible intelligence. The scientists like to put this alternatively as their faith in the natural laws that are a part of science itself.

Yet, the God has never been so redundant: even if He were to exist, the physicists see no need of God to interfere with the universe once. He has made the rules. This is so because the material principles seem to be working by themselves. God designed the universe in the form of a computer and natural laws in the form of software. There is no more any need of Him: since the creator has nothing novel anymore to create or safeguard.

Whether physicists agree or not, people at large invoke Him for His grace and mercy. Certainly, he may not be any incarnate God. But the immense complexity of the natural laws governing colossal universe makes man bow down his head to the power that may be that brought them into existence. As the power of human reason and intelligence unveils more and more of the secrets of the natural laws, man comes to appreciate better the endowment that has been bestowed upon him. Therefore, the Creator still endures as the spirit in the spirituality of man.

Albert Einstein (1879-1955) has said this in a poignantly simple letter written to a girl child. It was in the form of reply about what does a prayer mean to scientists. Asserting that the science looks towards validation of any phenomenon through the laws of nature, Einstein was intuitively sure of the fragmentary and imperfect nature of our present day knowledge of natural laws. He said that he had faith that there must be one unified field of knowledge, a spirit that manifests in the laws of nature that will encompass all knowledge[1]. In this letter, Einstein has also defined what a scientist's faith is as well as his religiosity (Appendix 1).

Thus, as science has much overwhelmed our civilization with spectacular validation in the form of empirical proofs, we tend to forget that there are other sources of knowledge and the fact that science has no exclusive patent in search for truth. Moreover, apart from the empirical sciences that pivot around the experimental proof that will answer in the form of true or false, there are other methods of scientific probing. Formal sciences working with abstract symbols illustrate this point well as they do arrive at logically valid and meaningful facts.

Though faith or intuition does not fall in any of the categories of science, yet, as Einstein asserts, they do form a gateway to truth. True as that may be, we are not going through that route over here. But, if truth were to be so unveiled, such a phenomenon or process does lead to inquiry through empirical methods. The present thesis is one such inquiry. And the empirical inquiry has to be by the tool of reason.

God endowed us with reason and having done so, He has left it to our intelligence to find a resolution to the riddle of the self and search for the Ultimate Reality*. Einstein thought there was a superhuman spirit—call that a god if you like—pervading the universe that regulated the laws of nature. On the other hand, most of the physicists, like Stephen Hawking (1942-2018) and Steven Weinberg (1933-), have found it not necessary to involve God in their search of Reality. This was also the case for Gautama Buddha who 2500 hundred years ago did not see the need to invoke any god as a creator and proclaimed that reason was sufficient for the human beings to guide them in their search as:

> O bhiksus and wise men, just as a goldsmith would test his gold by burning, cutting and rubbing it, so must you examine my words and accept them, but not merely out of reverence for me.[2]

The Present Proposition

It is proposed that the universe has an extra dimension incorporating consciousness. Each and every individual is a field of consciousness. As of today, we know four-dimensional space-time. Consciousness is continuously combined with space-time to give an additional dimension. So construed, the universe may be interpreted through the dimension of "space-time-consciousness continuum". We know that space-time dimension gets warped and there is frame dragging

---

* The definition of Reality has eluded us so far. Plato considered that we are chained men in a cave and our understanding of the world outside the cave is limited to our view of the shadows of the world that get reflected on the walls. Shankaracharya said almost the same thing with his classical statement that the perceptual world is unreal. As we shall see later, quantum reality has infinite possibilities.

too (*wide infra*). Undulations in the field of consciousness can further perturb this dimension to cause unusual occurrences in the perception of past, present and future. Such an interpretation will alter our everyday perception of the material world in the classical sense of space and time. The concept of "space-time-consciousness continuum" is referred here as Fifth Dimension.

The Method

This presentation attempts to explore the Reality of the universe and the concept of self through the parameters of space, time and consciousness. In the process, two alternative approaches for probing are juxtaposed. One approach is the modern scientific approach that examines the nature of the universe through the discoveries of physics and mathematics. The scientific facts regarding the self (as a seat of consciousness) are explored through the medium of psychology as well as the physiological understanding of the body and mind.

And the standard criteria for the modern scientific approach are that the facts so revealed are subject to further and future validation in the form of repeatable and reproducible experiments. It should be possible to quantify the facts. They should yield to the arguments of deductive logic and to inductive logic in a statistically significant measure. And there should always be a possibility of falsification or advancement of the thesis so arrived at, if that is to be considered scientific[3]. The scientific facts are generally supposed to be objective, i.e. without the interpretation by the investigator. However, the role of the observer has been widely debated in quantum physics. We shall see later on as to how far it is possible to be absolutely objective.

Starting with these premises, when we proceed to explore the nature of the Reality of our universe, we find the universe defined by the measurement of space, time and the observation of them through our consciousness. If space, time and consciousness are our tools, we have got to understand them precisely so as to interpret our results. We will first see how and what meaning the science has arrived at about these tools.

We shall then juxtapose the findings with the views and visions from the eastern traditions. For the validation of the metaphysical statements and concepts of the latter—paradoxical as it may seem—

we shall take recourse to the epistemological approach based on logical positivism*/empirical phenomena[4]. Of course, this does not produce statements that can be classified as true or false. However, an attempt is made to adduce empirical evidence and when that can be done, to assign such statements to scientific category. No mathematical proofs have been given; they do not exist so far in the realm of science of consciousness. It does not even yield to quantitative measurements.

While charting over this much-confusing area, every attempt is made to weed out the nonsensical so that even emotive and poetical, howsoever beautiful or profound it may seem, is excluded. Fraudulent practices abound in this area: they have no place for discussion here. Yet, the possibility of cognitive aberration is real and has been explored.

Even a single event, when found to be factual, should be taken as a phenomenon in nature that deserves to be explained.

In the process, the questions that such an occurrence raises are defined. Devoid of scientific explanation as per the understanding of the day, they are, then explored through the different parameters of space-time-consciousness.

ENDNOTES

1. Albert Einstein (1979). *The Human Side*, Princeton: Princeton University Press.
2. The Dalai Lama (1995). *The World of Tibetan Buddhism*, Boston, pp. 26, 160.
3. Karl Popper (1968). *The Logic of Scientific Discovery*, London.

* Logical positivism is a system of philosophy that clarifies the meaning of the statements, showing some to be scientific, some to be mathematical and others to be nonsensical. Every significant statement either is a statement of formal logic or is a statement of science. Rest is taken as nonsense.

2
Paranormal Occurrences

We have to explain the following:

(i) How the intuition—a product of faculty of refined consciousness—is generated.
(ii) The basis of the collective consciousness.
(iii) How the archetypes are the inheritance of the mankind.
(iv) The mystic experiences of the sages.
(v) Telepathy, precognition, clairvoyance, clairaudience and psychokinesis, poltergeist phenomena.
(vi) Near death experiences (NDE).
(vii) Hypnotic phenomena such as age regression and selective anesthesia of a certain block of the body*.
(viii) It does not have clear rational explanation for the practitioners of g-tummo-yoga who are able to raise their body temperatures to a high degree in subnormal climate[1].
(ix) Certain phenomena[2] like Whitten Effect and Bruce Effect that suggest a communion in consciousness.
(x) Reincarnation. Is it explainable? Or should this concept then be relegated to the class of superstition?
(xi) Déjà vu phenomenon.
(xii) Phenomena of transference and charisma.
(xiii) Paranormal healing.
(xiv) Abnormal survival; solar energy etc.

---

* In altered state of consciousness, it is possible to induce glove and stocking type of anesthesia, which is not localized by any anatomical criteria of nerve distribution. Raman Maharshi, a sage of South India, is documented to have his upper extremity amputated because of bone cancer without any anesthesia.

(xv) Materialization of objects and persons.

Most of these phenomena fall into the broad category of paranormal occurrences. Some may be labeled as extra-sensory perception. While a vast number of people are fascinated with them: they also fantasize about them. It is, therefore, very difficult to validate them. It is pertinent that we first see the arguments against them. They are:

1. Should the investigator not have personal experience of ESP?

Vasilev[3] carried out experiments at the Leningrad Institute for Brain Research for forty years (1924-1964). He collected factual descriptions of well-authenticated ESP incidences. This is criticized as analysis by a parapsychologist without having experience himself: it is also criticized that it falls in the category of heresy. Yes, validity may be better from those who know *psi* first hand. But, this is not a valid criticism for any scientific investigation. A scientist may not *experience* his data: only criterion should be that he should be following a scientific method.

2. The scientists studying ESP and paranormal phenomena provide pseudoscientific explanations. It is argued that there is lot of biased research by reasoning fallaciously.

We have tried to see that it does not happen. We shall follow the scientific parameters laid out concerning the method and the criteria for the elegant theory.

However, even a cursory look at the huge volume of literature[4] available in this arena would justify such criticism. The range is from sublime to ridiculous. To illustrate, there is an anecdote that describes Albert Einstein and Sigmund Freud collaborating in such an experiment. This was supposed to be an investigation about telepathy. And the success of the experiment was described as a medium having received a telepathic command from Freud to pull out three hairs from Einstein's moustache and executing it![5]

There is some scientific data available to us though it is very scanty. Earlier in the last century, there were several laudable efforts[6,8]. William Barrett, FRS (1844-1925) founded Society of

Psychical Research in London and short-lived American Society for Psychical Research. William McDougall, President of the Society for Psychical Research in 1920, believed that telepathy is very nearly established as a fact recognized by the science. However, he took the argument of negation by stating that nothing hitherto established by science or philosophy can be shown to imply that there is no spiritual life after death.

J.B. Rhine conducted research for six years at Dukes University in 1934. This consisted of highly controlled experiments; it could silence the criticism of research about the extrasensory phenomena. As a consequence, in 1937 *Journal of Parapsychology* was established. In 1940 the book *"Extrasensory perception after sixty years evidence"* was published. A large collection of data at the Dukes University was started in 1948[6]. One thousand cases were reported in 1953. While open criticism dropped off since then, it does not seem to have provided any fillip to research in the field.

On the other hand, there are skeptics who are interested to examine the data critically. Doubting as they are, Ray Hyman and McConnell[7] while following logical arguments for the rejection of ESP, assert that it is not fair to throw out every phenomenon as unscientific when it remains unexplained by the scientific methods of the present day.

It would then appear that the validation is not through more accumulation of the supportive data but only through a paradigm shift. That there is an additional dimension to the universe in the form of space-time-consciousness is the paradigm shift that we are defending now. If we can establish that paranormal phenomena do occur, then the only explanation that can support them has to be trans-personal, trans-spatial and trans-temporal.

3. Most intelligent persons would deny their own *psi* powers and suppress them. Psychic ability does not flourish among the well educated, particularly in Western cultures.

This cannot be helped. There will have to be a huge shift in values of our present civilization. But, the indications given by the development of humanistic and transpersonal schools of psychology are that a different paradigm is emerging.

4. The incidents of spontaneous ESP are infrequent, fleeting

and ambiguous; so they are impossible to be reproduced dependably.

This is genuine criticism as far as scientific study is concerned. Yes, ESP and paranormal occurrences cannot be generated at will. They just *happen.* But even a single event in the nature requires explanation by its eventuality. If it does happen, it cannot just be brushed aside because it is infrequent.

5. There is fraud in this arena particularly by those who are serving a clientele.

Yes, fraud is rampant and gullible people have fallen prey to it. But that can be easily exposed if subjected to investigation. Here the cliché is that most of the genuine people capable of such experiences are just not willing to be investigated: they do not have a point to make. Late in twentieth century, Dr. Kavoor of Sri Lanka declared a prize for anyone who can demonstrate a paranormal phenomenon. Even at present, James Brady*, a magician, has such a prize going; the difference is that now the sum is huge, a million dollars. Nobody has come to claim. There are journals devoted to expose fraud, Free Inquiry and Skeptical Inquirer, published by a society, *SCICOP.* The society works as the policeman of science. In spite of a very large following, the miracles, like the materialization of ashes from the hand of a famous saint in South India are shown as scientific trickery on the television shows. Monica's doctors question the miraculous cure of Monica by the recently beatified Mother Teresa. And there can be many such episodes. We have, therefore, restrained ourselves from cataloguing such events.

Stamping ground for the shamans: yes, so let us take care!

7. It creates double dualism.

ESP cannot be accounted by physics and physiology without adding an extra-physical dimension. To add an extra-physical component operating somewhere else so as to affect the physical creates enormous difficulties in assuming a non-biological control

* James Brady has challenged Uri Geller, the famous psychic. He has not accepted the challenge.

system. This is leading to double dualism—mind-body and mind-paranormal.

Any rational explanation should transcend this dualism[8]. Again, any explanation about causality of ESP should not violate the principle that there can be no causal connection between two events at different points in space if they are further apart than the distance that light can travel within the time interval between two events*. The interpretation of the consciousness as a quantum electro-dynamic field concurs with these parameters.

Justification for a Good Hypothesis

The present thesis is just an attempt to reconcile the various objections. It subscribes to rules of theory building and epistemological principles. It also advocates that statistical probabilities can lead to a theory. A theoretical construct regarding ESP and paranormal phenomena should also conform[9] to what is laid down as the criteria for justification of a good theory.

Let us elucidate these points in reference to paranormal phenomena in some detail.

1. Insight, Intuition, Inspiration, Creativity and Aesthetics

There are different connotations to the words. A hunch or intuition arises in the mind without a rational didactic process. There is no logical validation immediately, nor any logical steps. That way intuition differs from any irrational belief by the fact that it comes out as a future event or a fact: while superstitions are soon belied.

The most famous instance of intuition is Archimedes' Eureka. The Greek king was suspicious that his crown was not made of pure gold. He asked Archimedes to find out within a time limit, without breaking his crown and under the threat of a death penalty. Archimedes did not know how and was tormented. Under acute

---

* Further research about subatomic particles indicates that there may be particles—tachyons that travel at higher than the speed of light. This is to be further established. If consciousness is a QED, it can then translate as some subatomic particle. What would the property of consciousness particle—let us call it "conscion", be? Would it be like a photon or would it transcend the speed of light and qualify to be called a tachyon?

pressure thus, he sat in his bathtub and water overflowed. He ran through the streets naked, straight to the palace, shouting Eureka. He knew he had now only to compare the weight of pure gold displacing a certain amount of water with that of the crown. Archimedes was in the altered state of consciousness when he got the intuitive answer.

These refined qualities of intellect may reflect fields with higher potentials. The evidence is only indirect. It is a common knowledge that generation of insight is not accomplished by any amount of toil that goes in the process of didactic, dialectic, and discursive logic. This is restricted to the left hemisphere functioning of the brain. Insight strikes like a flesh of lightening. Poetical truth and justice are experienced by the mankind since ages but may not qualify as empirical evidence. There are several notable examples in the field of science. Discovery of benzene ring by Kekule through a dream is interesting. He dreamt of serpents forming a ring by holding each other at the tail end. So did Singer dream of spears with a hole at the proximal end, to invent the sewing needle. The latest is the discovery of DNA code by Watson and Crick. To quote Watson[10]:

> When I got to our still empty office the next day morning, I quickly cleared away the papers from my desktop so I would have a large, flat surface on which to form pairs of bases held together by hydrogen bonds.... I saw all too well that my prejudices led nowhere.... Then I saw that both pairs could be flip-flopped over...

There are several illustrative examples of mathematical geniuses. The living personality of Shakuntala Devi computes faster than a computer. The arguments against her can be that she has a brain that itself is faster than a computer; she does not have any original contribution. But Fermat's last theorem is a better example. Fermat was a soldier engaged in combat and wrote the formula while in a trench. Battle began before he could write the proof. The paper was found in the trench by the side of his dead body. While the theorem held good in mathematics, several years lapsed before a British mathematician won the Field's medal (equivalent to Nobel Prize) for solving it and Andre Weil at Princeton University also derived the proof recently. The story of the mathematician Ramanujan goes a step further. Had it not been for G.H. Hardy, this formally uneducated genius probably would have never been found. The mathematical formulae that he arrived at were most extraordinary. When questioned, his answer was that Devi of Namakkal (a goddess of worship at his village) appears to him in his dreams and he writes them down in the morning! And further to this, there is a time-honored model—Einstein.

Einstein's Letter: A Model

Einstein describes the experience of intense creativity through insight and intuition in response to a query from Hadamard[11]. Einstein has admitted to getting into a different state of mind in his creative moments. He has described it as thinking with the symbols. This is reproduced verbatim as:

My Dear Colleague,

In the following, I am trying to answer in brief your questions as well as I am able. I am not satisfied myself with those answers and I am willing to answer more questions if you believe this could be of any advantage for the very interesting and difficult work you have undertaken.

(a) The words or the language, as they are written or spoken, do not seem to play any role in my mechanism of thought. The psychical entities, which seem to serve as elements in thought are certain signs and more or less clear images that can be "voluntarily" reproduced and combined.

There is, of course, a certain connection between those elements and relevant logical concepts. It is also clear that the desire to arrive finally at logically connected concepts is the emotional basis of this rather vague play with the above-mentioned elements. But taken from a psychological viewpoint, this combinatory play seems to be the essential feature in productive thought—before there is any connection with logical construction in words or other kind of signs that can be communicated to others.

(b) The above-mentioned elements are, in my case, of visual and some muscular type. Conventional words or other signs have to be sought for laboriously only in a secondary stage, when the mentioned associative play is sufficiently established and can be reproduced at will.

(c) According to what has been said, the play with the mentioned elements is aimed to be analogous to certain logical connections one is searching for.

(d) Visual and motor. In a stage when words intervene at all, they are, in my case, purely auditive, but they interfere only in a secondary stage as already mentioned.

(e) It seems to me that what you call full consciousness is a limit case that can never be fully accomplished. This seems to be connected with the fact called the narrowness of consciousness.

Revelation from a Background State

Penrose[12] conjures a background state of silent activity at such moments of insight. This is based on his own experience. After detailed discussion about the possibilities of various physical designs of the process of consciousness, he explores the field of intuition that leads to fascinating discussion of consciousness at the moment of mathematical discoveries. He describes a moment of flash while his conversation stopped with his colleague at the time of crossing a street. He had solved a mathematical problem concerning the center of black hole in his mind in that short time that was perplexing him for quite a while. But on resumption of conversation after the street was crossed, he forgot all about it. However, he continued to feel a strange feeling of elation around him. He had to chase that feeling for quite a while as to what its cause could be till he realized that the cause was the sudden resolution of a long-standing riddle.

And there are many such other instances from ordinary life too. The fact that the insights came without didactic, dissective, dialectic reasoning does say something about an extraordinary occurrence. It is not possible to tap such an event at will. Even if it is an altered state of consciousness, we can only deduce that such an alternate/ differential/quantum jump in processing does occur in the brain.

Insight can be in the nature of self-reflection: it may be a look within oneself. Generation of insight into ones personality is a standard modality of all forms of psychotherapy. Jung created a model of insight generation by having a dialogue with an imaginary person. Jung described this as transcendental function that served as a tool in all forms of creativity and healing.

Numinous Images and Guiding Angels

Jung's subjects experienced a kind of luminosity during transcendent imagination. The numinous images came up in these subjects spontaneously and their spiritual quality made Jung to think that this was a way to connect to divinity or God. Some of the most interesting examples of the creative process through imagery show the generation of ecstatic states and heightened insight that are familiar in the literature of mysticism[13]. Jose Silva[14] has popularized his "mind control" method where he employs a councillor. But in contrast to numinous images that Jung's subjects experienced, Silva may employ the image of Sophia Loren! What is of relevance is a dialogue that one establishes with such images that leads to insight generation to resolve ones conflicts. We have been using this technique for psychotherapy and employ such images that suit the subject's sensibilities. The process does require reinforcement and the insight may not occur as instantaneous flash; but eventually it does arise either as a flash or a gentle trickle of a ray of light.

Penrose attributes such flashes to the activities of unconscious mind. His use of the word unconscious mind is a misnomer here. Let us see how? Is it an exploration of unconscious mind? Unconscious mind stores what it has already known, found repugnant and has repressed. It cannot provide generic ground for something fresh and new that is the essential feature of creativity and invention. It is evidently clear that this is not the function of ordinary state of consciousness. More often than not, unconscious mind deals with ugly things that need to be repressed and need be relegated to the dark recesses of mind. Instead there is another cue in his description that will take us further. That is about his feeling of elation.

Truth is Beauty and Beauty is Joy

Elation is a feeling of being "high". Like Penrose, Heisenberg has also described this feeling on the discovery of Uncertainty Principle[15]. Perhaps everyone has experienced such elation once in a while. Who does not feel "high", when face to face with a reality that is transcendental? A discovery or invention is creativity incarnated and it takes one in direct confrontation with a new dimension of reality. Reality so experienced is beauty personalized and a thing of beauty is a joy for ever. From an entity that is not quantifiable, the consciousness, we are led to further abstract realms of aesthetics. The most ardent and unabashed advocacy for the equivalence of a good theory to a thing of beauty comes from Dirac[16] who is the youngest Nobel Laureate so far and (therefore) has the largest number of his students to receive Nobel Prize. He claims that it was his keen sense of beauty that enabled him to *divine* (the word is as used by Dirac) his equation for the electron. That is because Truth is beauty and beauty is joy*.

So intuition is not just a delayed recall. Nor is it plumbing or ploughing of the unconscious. It seems to arise from a background state of silent rumination over a problem for a length of time. Let us consider each moment of reflection as a generation of a single QED. Progressing in an algorithm, several such fields then superimpose to arrive in a flash. Intuition thus is said to be the product of the super-impositions of several QEDs.

We have arrived at a step where we can now conceive intuition as a creative endeavour. What is of further relevance is that such a processing is facilitated by altered state of consciousness/ meditation. While one cannot cultivate intuition so as to reveal itself at will, it can at least be approached through meditation. This is to be discussed later.

2. & 3. Collective Consciousness and Archetypal Symbols

Archetypal symbols signify the memory of a herd. They manifest repeatedly in group actions.[17]. Where from the information is derived? Jung ascribes it to dynamic demiurgic forces in the collective unconscious mind. But where is the collective unconscious mind? Where does it reside and how does it operate? The tremendous appeal of the archetypal symbols to the masses is well known. The classic example is the national flag. That may be explained as gross conditioning of the mind. But the influence of archetypal symbols is seen to be deeply pervasive not only in a cultural group but in entire human race as can be seen from the dream contents.

---

* (cf. with the concept of *sat-chit-ananda,* meaning Truth-consciousness-bliss as *a* primordial expression of Reality in Indian Classical tradition discussed later.)

A singular image is explainable on the basis of the brain function. But, if consciousness is unitary, confined to the single hardware of one individual brain, there can be no collective consciousness or collective unconscious mind. The collective unconscious would be just a myth, and archetypes would be aberrant images whose collective appeal cannot be explained. If there is a collective basis to consciousness, we do not know how that can be explained by the materialist philosophy. However, consciousness as QED field may explain it as the confluence of fields in various individuals.

Some laboratory data is available which validates such a hypothesis to some extent. Nagendra and co-researchers[18] at Vivekanand Yoga Research Foundation have found that in two of the several groups that they studied, the group offering prayers at Ramazan and one other prayer group did influence the Random Event Generator (REG). They also noted that the intent of the subjects under study as well as the practice of cyclical meditation also influenced REG. They also note that their findings are similar to that of a consortium—Princeton Engineering Anomalies Research (PEAR) Laboratory, Friedburg Anomalous Mind Machine Interaction group (FAMMI) and Giessen Anomalies Research Project (GARP).

4. *Mystic Experiences of Sages*

We have known Dilip Kumar Roy personally. He was a famous musician of the last century. He has described several such experiences pertaining to himself in his books.[19,20] We shall mention just two.

At a music concert in the Himalayas, he went to see a sage out of curiosity. Waking from the meditative state, the sage told him that his *guru* who lived in South India would call him. Roy rushed down to Pondicherry to be told by Sri Aurobindo, a mystic saint of last century, that his time had not come yet and that he would call him at an appropriate time. Roy went on giving music concerts till once on a boat in the Mediterranean Sea, at night he felt "the call". Next day he changed his course, went back to India and Sri Aurobindo told him that he had sent the "call". He stayed over for good.

Before Mahatma Gandhi's assassination, Roy had a vision of the event as it did happen. He wrote it down and sent to the

Government of India. It was ignored. Gandhi was murdered as described by Roy.

The events are rare, unusual, and not so frequent but they certainly are not pranks. They are honest accounts by a person belonging to microscopic minority-sages.

That raises another question: what is the difference between the visions of these sages and madmen? Peter Heaths[21], who is a lifetime inmate of the Pondicherry Ashram, in fact, carried an investigation in the psychohistory of well-researched schizophrenics and the madmen of God. He tabulated the personality, character and the visions of two schizophrenics, viz. Daniel Paul Scheher[22] and Madeleine Le Bouc[23] and compared their traits against those of Sri Aurobindo,* who was known to have visions. He also thought he was influencing the world events through his yoga. According to Heaths, many of the traits of Sri Aurobindo, including his parentage, suggested similarities between him and the psychotics. However, taking recourse to the well founded medical criteria that a madman is so disoriented from the reality that he is not able to engage in any meaningful interaction with his environment, Heaths stresses the point that Sri Aurobindo in his everyday life was well connected with close associates, was creative and did enjoy humour.

What shall we arrive at from this? The inference that we wish to highlight is the fact that mystics live in a different mode of consciousness (Chapter 5). But they have the faculty of ordinary perception and cognition in tact. Their conceptualization can also be intelligently meaningful. This different state of consciousness is called the Fourth State—*turya* (meaning fourth) in classical Indian tradition. Sri Aurobindo called it overmind.

Without collapsing into ridiculous from the sublime realms of mysticism, it is pertinent to mention a worldwide happening. Jose

---

* Sri Aurobindo failed himself in Indian Civil Service examination when he did not appear for the customary horse-riding test, which was just a formality. English-educated from childhood, he came over to Baroda, India at the instance of the then Maharaja of Baroda. He was active in freedom struggle till 1907. He was initiated in meditative practice in 1905 at Baroda and migrated to French enclave of Pondicherry in 1910. He coined the word "overmind" state for the altered state of consciousness at which the meditation just begins. He was a modern mystic, who integrated four systems of *yoga* in Indian tradition. His magnum opus is *Savitri*, an epic poem.

Silva, a mystic who has devised a 48-hour course for special training of the mind—The Silva Mind Control Method—claims many near miracles. One such spectacular event may be the winning at a lottery!*

Silva was barely a literate man. Yet he claims to have lectured at most prominent universities in the world. And he is the author of *The Method* and one of the best selling psychology book[24]. The man somehow learnt to manipulate his dreams and had vision of a magic number 3-4-3 followed by 3-7-3. Not only that but some strange occurrences took him to a store where he saw his dream numbers on a lottery ticket. He won the lottery (*vide supra*, memories of future and stock market). He imparts his mind control programme at a fee and claims four of his "graduates" have won lotteries utilizing his techniques. An impressive list of people with Ph.D. and M.D. decorate his acknowledgements.

If Silva was not fooling many people at many, many times at so many places, is there an explanation? There has to be a trans-personal, trans-spatial and trans-temporal phenomenon to explain this. If consciousness were to be a QED field, there might be a possible explanation. It will still leave open the scope for the further exploration of this field.

The reason this is mentioned here is that considering whatever that is claimed by Mr. Silva as probable, his method utilizes the fourth state of consciousness. At this stage we would like to mention that fourth state of consciousness is the gateway to the fifth dimension where the conventional space-time dimension takes a quantum jump into five dimensional, space-time-consciousness continuum. Let us have a further glimpse of that dimension through the innocence of childhood when the consciousness has the pristine pure quality away from the projections of mind.

5. *Telepathy, Précognition, Clairvoyance, Clairaudience, Psychokinesis, Poltergeist Phenomena*† [25]

They occur so infrequently in routine life that they have news value

* It is not only our firm belief but a universally acclaimed view amongst the believers of mysticism that one cannot turn to the Fourth State of consciousness as well as "get entry" to the Fifth Dimension, space-time-consciousness, for selfish ends.

† There is disturbance in the environment of an adolescent who is being suppressed and feels suffocation. There is breaking of the glass

in media. There are journals devoted to investigate these aspects like *Journal of Parapsychology and International Journal of Parapsychology*. We do not intend to catalogue such events. But the emphasis is that such events do occur. Our emphasis is that they occur when the subject is in the altered state of consciousness. For such a state to spontaneously occur, the children are the most sensitive grounds since their minds are likely to be uncorrupted. The other necessary condition seems to be close emotional bond. Thomas Armstrong[26] describes an incident as:

> This event happened when I was sitting in my house and the idea came to me that my maternal uncle was involved in an accident and had died. A telegram was received the same evening intimating the death of my uncle. This happened at a long distance from here, when my uncle was driving a taxi.

A Canadian psychiatrist personally told us the following:

> I was in my bedroom at about 2.00 a.m. when I suddenly woke up and felt drawn to the balcony of my bedroom. It was freezing cold. Yet, I moved over to the balcony. Once there, I felt the presence of my father who hugged me close to him. After a while, the feeling departed and I went to bed uneasy. Next day I came to know that my father had died around the same time, several thousand miles away in India.

A person has told us personally. The person is Dr. Sudhir Shah (who has investigated Hirachand Manek and Prahlad Jani as discussed later). As a student in the college, he could see the question papers in his dreams. He could foretell what was about to happen to some of his close friends. But he was in for a shock when one day CBI knocked at his door. This was following his prediction to some friends that a certain prime minister was to be assassinated and the person was indeed killed. Of course, CBI found no criminality but thereafter, Dr. Shah talked about these matters only with certain reluctance.

And there are stories in our own personal lives similar to above. The story of precognition of a kind, running in the family, pertains

---

and knocking off the books of the shelf by "unseen" forces. Such occurrences are termed poltergeist phenomena (*vide infra*).

to the academic examinations. In the college days, one of us (BV) used to have images of questions a few hours before examination and would tell his friends what was to be asked. They even thought he had leaked the papers. This ran in the family so that one of our daughters too saw the question papers and, the *viva voce* questions would occur to her a few hours before the event. One of our grand-children can, many a times, speak aloud what his mother has been thinking at that moment. But, this is spontaneous and cannot be conducted as an experiment.

Some of the famous parapsychology events are that of Peter Hercose, Uri Geller and Mathew Manning[27]. Peter had ESP to discover lost items and his most notable achievement was to retrieve the stone of Scotland that is traditionally kept under the throne of British monarch. BBC ran a television series of shows where Uri demonstrated his ability to bend spoons and mend watches. This inspired several children who repeated the feats. Manning had the same kind of ability to affect psychokinesis.

The noted child psychologist, Jean Piaget, explains the psychic events in children. He ascribes such a possibility to the ability of the mind to entertain any state in a continuum of possible states as equally valid and return to the point from which the operation of the mind begins. The phrase, continuum of possible states, equates nearly to the quantum electro-dynamic fields. Memory is now understood as a state dependent condition of the entire memory coding and transmitting apparatus in the body. We conjecture that the state is in the form of a field. But Jean Piaget is no more to clarify.

The reason this is mentioned is to state that parapsychology is enough of an event. Its physicality has not been explained by the physical sciences. Having stated the position *vis-à-vis* the altered state of consciousness, we now take the thesis a step ahead. The only way to explain such phenomena along with collective consciousness, as well as the importance of archetypal symbols, is to see consciousness as the energy in a wave/field form; a wave/field that has no particulate matter incorporated, or may be, has subatomic particles of the size of photon (0 mass). Such a wave will travel at the speed of light. But this wave shall have the properties that can propel it across physical barriers of various kinds to explain some of the most remarkable data.

Let us examine one such evidence from theosophical literature. The literature under review here is gigantic, a monumental evidence about clairvoyance that may be explained as a natural outcome of the Fifth Dimension. At the same time, the evidence is historical. The limitation is that none of the personalities are alive today. And no other member of the Theosophical Society repeats it.

The founder of the Society, Madame Blavatsky took C.W. Leadbeater and Annie Besant in her tutelage. They were also initiated into what may be called occult practices. From our* review of the theosophical literature, we are inclined to surmise that they practiced some form of Mahayana Buddhist meditation. It is also said they were initiated into *kundalini* yoga†. And as we mentioned earlier, meditation is a process that progresses in the fourth state of consciousness: that leads to advanced states of consciousness and opens up the vision to the Fifth Dimension. It is essentially a spiritual endeavor. But, as a consequence of the additional dimensionality, some extraordinary phenomena are observed. One of them is *anima*. It literally means ability to see the minutest. The Sanskrit description is as follows:

Pravrtty-aloka-nyasat suksma-vyavahita-viprakrsta-jnanam[28]

It literally translates as, (a yogi can acquire) "knowledge of the small, the hidden or the distant by directing the light of super physical faculty". Putting it simply, it means that one can extend the powers of perception. Through such a projection one can cognize the small, the hidden and the distant. This is tantamount to micro sensing. Empowered thus, C.W. Leadbeater and Annie Besant set out to decipher the ultimate nature of the material elements. The accounts and the results of their experiments appear in a monumental work, Occult Chemistry[29]. When they started their experiments in 1895, they seemed to be impressed by the Periodic Table of chemical elements as propounded by Sir William Crookes (1832-1919). When they set out to investigate the Ultimate Particle, i.e. Atom according to the perception of their time, in the last decade of the nineteenth century, Rutherford (1871-1937) had not yet deciphered the structure of the atom. However, the Periodic Table of the chemical elements had been worked out. This was reminiscent of the design argument that tallied with their philosophical mode.

---

* The authors are theosophists: but their approach is not devotional. Theosophy teaches, true to the Buddhist tradition, to be critical.

† This form of *yoga* is discussed later on.

The work contains the observations and results of the experiments carried out across a span of forty years, from 1895 to 1933. The method of investigation was to diminish one's own conception of oneself to the minutest level. As a consequence, when they observed an atom, it appeared highly magnified. Their Tibetan Gurus belonging to Mahayana lineage taught this to them. Explaining this, Jinarajadasa[98] says:

> Just as a microscopist looking into the microscope and without removing his eyes from the slide, can describe what he observes so that it can be recorded, so the clairvoyant investigator watching an atom or molecule can describe what he sees in front of him, What he sees is not subjective, in the sense that it is a creation of the imagination: it is objective as is the paper on which I am writing this and the pen which I use.

The first investigations were made in England in 1895 utilizing micro *psi* perception. Four gases were observed. They were Hydrogen, Oxygen, Nitrogen a nd a fourth gas (atomic weight = 3) till then not discovered by the chemists. Thereafter, at periodic intervals, the results were published in *The Theosophist* up to 1934.

The results, to say the least, are spectacular. They "saw" that the elements were made up of "*Anu**" which, according to them was the smallest particulate matter, smaller than the atom. They called it ultimate physical atom—UPA. *Anu* existed in two varieties, positive and negative, and in its formation the spirals wound themselves in opposite directions (Fig. 5). Say, Hydrogen was made up of 18 *Anu*. (They did not ascribe plural to *Anu*). They described isotopes five years before they were known to science and English Chemist Frederick Soddy (1877-1956) gave the name as isotope† to the atoms of an element differing in mass. They visualized the structure of diamond, composed of 594 atoms and a model was also made and the photographs published in *The Theosophist*.

The matter becomes more evident in reference to the studies by Stephen Phillips.[30,31] He is a physicist and taught at University of California after obtaining his Ph.D. at his *alma mater*. Phillips has

---

* *Anu* is a Sanskrit word meaning a small particle.

† Isotopes have the same number of protons in their nucleus but differing number of neutrons.

studied the results of micro-*psi* investigations for 20 years and came to the remarkable conclusion that they are indeed extrasensory perceptions at micro level. He discounts the possibility of fraud as well as precognition. Some of the findings were a few years ahead of the scientific publication of the same data. Totally, 91 elements were so studied; some of them were not even detected by science at that particular time. In 1909 they recorded an element, technetium and described it again in 1932. Even then it was five years ahead of its discovery by science. Such wealth of information abounds in Occult Chemistry that it 1951, third edition contained descriptions of 111 atoms of elements, including 14 isotopes and the molecules of 29 inorganic compounds and 22 organic compounds. According to Phillips, the description goes beyond the atomic level: it extends to subatomic particles, quarks, and sub-quark as well as to strings. Phillips tabulates (Table 2.1) the data that is illuminating. The incidence of the error between micro-*psi* calculations and the scientific data is negligible. In most cases the error percentage is zero: where there is, it is around 1 per cent.

Table 2.1: Chronology of Micro-***psi*** Experiments and Scientific Discoveries

Year Micro-psi	*Science*
1895 positive and negative hydrogen triplets observed in MPAs*	1964 Quark model proposes nuclei are made up of 2 positive u quarks and 1 negative d quark and also in reverse mode
1908 meta-neon (number weight = 22.33);	1912 Neon-22 discovered
1908 axes of UPAs** observed to be aligned by electric field; UPAs depicted as joined by lines of force of a magnetic nature;	1933 magnetic monopoles with possible electric dipole moments discussed by Dirac
1908 some UPAs shown as end points of single lines of force	1970s String model of hadrons; quarks regarded as ends of strings or flux tubes
1908 Y shaped configurations of lines of force ending on UPA published 1909 "illinium" (number weight = 146.66);	1975 Baryons modeled as Y-shaped strings with quarks at their ends 1945 promethium-147 discovered
1909 "masurium" (number weight = 100.11)	1937 technitium-99 discovered
1924 processional motions of 'hydrogen triangles' (protons)	1924 spin of nuclei suggested
1932 element 85 (number weight = 221.00); element 87 (number weight 222.55)	1940 astatine 219 discovered 1939 francium 223 discovered.

* Mirco-*Psi* Atom—It is used by occultist chemists. Not synonymous with modern nomenclature.

** UPAs stands for Ultimate Physical Atoms.

Considering the spectacular nature of this micro-sensing, Srinivasan[32] remarks:

> Those of us who have...scrutinized both the original observations as recorded by Besant and Leadbeater... and the remarkable interpretation of the same in terms of the most up-to-date concepts of contemporary particle physics...cannot but be overawed by the minuteness and depth to which Besant and Leadbeater appear to have been able to delve into the intricacies of the structure of the matter.

Micro-sensing in Jain Tradition

The above phenomena are only a century old. The prophet of Jain religion, Mahavir was born about 2500 years ago and Jain and Buddhist traditions are more or less contemporaries. Both the traditions generated an occult discipline*. There is immaculate description of atoms and sub-atomic particles in the books[33,34] of Jain tradition too. The original books are by Umasvati and Hemchandracharya. The texts are a thousand years old. The recently published versions give original *Pali* version and its translation†. In the translations of this kind, there are definite possibilities of differences in semantic interpretation. But we put the historical data concerning the modern scientific discoveries as text that may be corresponding to the interpretation of the Jain tradition.

The Elementary Particles in Jain Philosophical Texts

1. Pudgal is matter (*pud*) and yet it disappears (*galan*) and is the smallest of the small particles of matter. 2. That consciousness which is non-dual is also *pudgal*. 3. By the union of *pudgals* with each other, the gross matter arises. 4. Though *pudgal* is beyond the definition of origin, middle or end, since it has a charge (*ekpradeshi*),

---

* Jain occultism was also rooted in a form of meditation that has come to be known as *preksha* meditation. That these visions were perceived in a meditative state is derived from a quote from the referred text that says they are observed in a state of *nirvikalpa samadhi.*

† This is further substantiated by personal discussions with an erudite Jain Muni, Kirti Chandra Maharaj at Tithal, Valsad, Gujarat, India.

it can be said to have a direction. 5. *Pudgal* is one that cannot be pierced or divided by the sharpest instrument and one that cannot be destroyed. 6. By the combination of eight subtle (*sannasana*) sub-particles, one *pudgal* is produced. 7. *Pudgal* may exist as a particle or a field. 8. By the dissolution of a combination (*skandha*), that indivisible element which is obtained is the active *pudgal*. 9. From the coming together of various *pudgals*, a combination (*skandha*) is brought about. 10. *Pudgals* with flavor and color are described and they change themselves from one state to another. 11. A *pudgal* is not inactive; it exists in a dynamic state. 12. In one space only a single *pudgal* can exist. But if it is paired, the pair may exist in a single location in space. *Pudgal* has property to combine; that shows that it is active.

The infinitely vast space and the infinitesimal small *pudgal* are two expressions of the same reality.

Historical Data Concerning Modern Physics

In 1924, de Broglie (1894-1987) described the theory of wave particle duality for which he was awarded Nobel Prize in 1929. An electron, when detached from the atom, is called free electron and free electron theory treats electrons as freely moving. What is consciousness is not understood in physics so far. It is non-quantifiable. Protons and electrons were discovered by the beginning of 20th century and in 1932, Neutrons were discovered as the fundamental constituents of matter. According to quantum theory as postulated by Planck (1858-1947), elementary particles have a spin in a particular direction. This won him Nobel Prize in 1918. Strong nuclear force, responsible for holding together of positively charged protons and neutral neutrons was postulated in 1930 and established in 1940. Yukava (1907-1981), a Japanese physicist, predicted in 1930 that there is a fundamental force holding the nucleus of an atom together. He called it a "middle weight" before it was termed as meson. The nuclear force between protons and neutrons is termed strong nuclear interaction. Gel Mann (1929-) in 1964 proposed the eightfold way to define the structure of particles. The basic principle of quantum theory says that a subatomic particle may be a particle or field. Hadrons are a class of subatomic particles. They are made of quarks. Various combinations of quarks constitute matter. In 1978, a standard model

Table 2.2: Micro-*psi* visualization of the Elementary Particles in Jain philosophical texts[94,95] and corresponding scientific data

1. That which is matter (*pud*) and yet it disappears (*galan*). is the smallest of the small particle of matter (*pudgal*).	In 1924, de Broglie (1894-1987) described the theory of wave particle duality for which he was awarded Nobel prize in 1929. An electron when detached from the atom, it is called free electron and free electron theory treats electrons as freely moving.
2. That consciousness which is non-dual is also *pudgal*.	Not established in physics so far. Consonant with our hypothesis that consciousness is a field and an additional dimension.
3. By the union of *pudgal* with each other, the gross matter arises.	Protons and electrons were discovered by the beginning of 20th century and in 1932, neutrons were discovered as the fundamental constituents of matter.
4. Though *pudgal* is beyond the definition of origin, middle or end, since it has a charge (*ekpradeshi*), it can be said to have a direction.	According to quantum theory as postulated by Planck (1858-1947), Elementary Particles have a spin in a particular direction. This won him Nobel Prize in 1918.
5. One that cannot be pierced or divided by the sharpest instrument, and one that cannot be destroyed.	Strong nuclear force, responsible for holding together of positively charged protons and neutral neutrons was postulated in 1930 and established in 1940.
6. By the combination of eight subtle (*sannasana*) sub-particles, one *pudgal* is produced.	Yukava (1907-1981), a Japanese physicist predicted in 1930 that there is a fundamental force holding the nucleus of an atom together. He called it a "middle weight" before it was termed as meson. The nuclear force between protons and neutrons is termed strong interaction. Gel Mann (1929-) in 1964 proposed the eightfold way to define the structure of particles.
7. *Pudgal* may exist as a particle or a field.	This is the basic principle of quantum theory. See Schrodinger's cat Experiment and Heisenberg's Uncertainty Principle discussed above.
8. By the dissolution of a combination (*skandha*), that indivisible element which is obtained, is the active *pudgal*.	Hadrons are a class of subatomic particles. They are made of quarks.
9. From the coming together of various *pudgals*, a combination (*skandha*) is brought about.	There are various combinations of quarks that constitute matter. In 1978, a standard model for the constitution of all matter was established as that of leptons,* quarks and mediators.

10. *Pudgals* with flavor and color are described and they change themselves from one state to another.	Quarks combine with each other through affinity that is determined by 'color charge'. The theory governing these color charge combinations is called quantum Chromo-dynamics. Various 'flavors' are also ascribed to quarks*. These advances have occurred between 1961-64-74-78-1998.
11. A *pudgal* is not inactive; it exists in a dynamic state.	Subatomic particles are ascribed a particular spin.
12. In one space only a single *pudgal* can exist. But if it is paired, the pair may exist in a single location in space.	Pauli's (1900-58) exclusion principle formulated in 1924-25, states that no two identical particles in a system can exist in the same space. He won the Nobel prize in 1945. Dirac (1902-84) derived the equation that postulated existence of a positron —anti-electron in 1927. They have the same mass but opposite charge. He won the Nobel prize in 1933. Youngest to win the prize so far, he has to his credit largest number of his students winning the prize.
13. *Pudgal* has property to combine, that shows that it is active.	See 8, 9, 10 above.
14. The infinitely vast space and the infinitesimal small *pudgal* are two expressions of same reality.	Space is supposed to be filled with infinite energy field; a small undulation in this field materializes the matter (*vide supra*).

for the constitution of all matter was established as that of leptons*, quarks and mediators.

Quarks combine with each other through affinity that is determined by 'color charge'. The theory governing these color charge combinations is called quantum chromo-dynamics. Various 'flavors' are also ascribed to quarks†. These advances have occurred in 1961-64, 1974-78: and in 1998. Subatomic particles are ascribed a particular spin. Pauli's (1900-1958) exclusion principle formulated in 1924-25, states that no two identical particles in a system could exist in the same space. He won the Nobel Prize in 1945. Dirac (1902-84) derived the equation that postulated existence of a positron—anti-electron in 1927. They have the same mass but opposite charge. He won the Nobel Prize in 1933. Space is supposed to be filled with

* Lepton means light in weight. These are electron, muon and nutrino.

† Colour and flavors that are ascribed to quarks are entirely descriptive. It should be obvious that they are not the sensory qualities.

infinite energy field; a small undulation in this field materializes the matter.

The data is significant to our thesis. It shows that there is a dimension different from our ordinary perception. Such a perception can give accurate description of physical reality. This dimension is accessible through some form of meditation. Recently, objective evidence about the neuro-regeneration and development of centers in the frontal lobe of the brain is available.[35]

Poltergeist Phenomena[36]

They are fairly uncommon kind of unusual experiences around the adolescents. There are unexplainable crashes of the contents of the young child's home environment. There may be knocking off the books of the shelves, crashing of the lamps and explosions. They seem to be occurring in an environment where an adolescent is experiencing a deep need to rebel. These "Para psychological" phenomena have not been frequent to be subjected to any detailed study. But Near Death Experiences are frequent and have been studied in children as well as adults.

6. Near Death Experiences (NDE)[37]

What happens when a person is "temporarily" dead? There are several instances when a person is almost dead, may be declared dead and he "returns". It is not uncommon now-a-days when, say during an operative session, the heart of a subject stops for less than three minutes and the subject is revived before he undergoes brain death. The unique feature of the NDE is the classical similarity in all such subjects. Such and other subjects who may have been comatose for some time tell the same story on lines similar to these:

> I stepped out and fell into the darkness. The next thing I was aware of was being up near the ceiling. The light was dim and I saw at first nothing unusual. Then I saw myself lying on the... (table, floor etc.). I was a little surprised but not at all upset at seeing myself that way...I saw that I was not moving at all. I said to myself, "I guess I am dead."...I was not afraid...I saw the dim light slowly going brighter...It was very bright and beautiful...It

> seemed to be at the end of a long tunnel which was getting brighter and brighter...I felt very happy...Then the light was gone...I felt groggy and sick and I woke up with a terrible headache.[37]

Reviewing the diverse data presented so far, we are left with the following. There are other states of consciousness than those, we ordinary are aware about; that there are empirical proofs available about a fourth state of awareness where paranormal phenomena seem to occur. The awareness of the material universe, through and beyond the fourth state appears to be entirely different from what we usually perceive.

7. Evidence of Age Regression

We have seen the evidence of age regression in hypnosis earlier. Now let us raise some questions.

There are instances when the age is said to have regressed up to intrauterine age. In one instance, a person was having phobia about sharp objects. He was regressed to the intrauterine age of 10 weeks. He "saw" a sharp object approaching "itself". The subject underwent catharsis at this point and the session was terminated with suitable post-hypnotic suggestions. The mother of the subject when interrogated admitted to having undergone an attempt at abortion at about that time. The phobia of the subject was gone. The relevant question is: did the embryo have consciousness at the age of 10 weeks? Is that consciousness capable of perceiving the material world around "itself"? Does this consciousness arise out of chemical reactions and at what age? Or does the consciousness exist somewhere else and get incorporated into the embryo? If so, at what age? If the consciousness was somewhere else, where was "it" and in what state?

Science does not have the answers. Whatever answer is there is only on the material basis that the fertilized ovum undergoes development and in the process at some stage, the molecular biological events progress to a stage when the embryo becomes conscious. The probable age will correspond with the development of the nervous system between 8 to 12 weeks of intrauterine age.

8. Selective Anesthesia

The scientific "wired loop to the central telephone exchange" model cannot explain a selective block anesthesia that can be produced in hypnosis. In such an instance, a certain part of the body is totally numb, irrespective of its nerve distribution. With the use of local anesthetic drugs, the doctors block selective nerves, which is akin to cutting off a telephone temporarily by blocking its connection. But the anesthesia, in such instances, is naturally confined to the distribution of the nerve so blocked. It is not so under hypnosis*. It blocks the sensation in an area irrespective of its nerve distribution. The studies of such anaesthetized part show that the changes that accompany the perception of pain in a given part do occur: what is blocked is the perception of the pain at conscious level in the brain*.

G-tummo-yoga

G-tummo yoga[38] is a form of Tibetan yogic practice. The adepts sit in subnormal temperatures in the open with their body bare. They go into an altered state, a form of meditation when their body temperature starts rising. They do compete with other practitioners as to how many sheets they could dry in a specified time. The Dalai Lama facilitated Herbert Benson, a Harvard physician to study such monks. Benson published his findings in various journals and a book, *The Relaxation Response.*

Herbert Benson noted that the young monks would raise their body temperature in the state of G-tummo-yoga, so much so that the body would feel warm when the outside temperature is zero or sub-zero. They would then take the wet sheets of clothes soaked in ice-cold water and apply it on their bodies. The normal sense perception is through the body to the brain. Here the brain orders the body to do otherwise and the sense perception differs completely from the material world.

Whitten Effect and Bruce Effect

Whitten Effect is observed in the females living in dormitory in

* We have conducted experiments to show hypno-anaesthesia. We have done surgical operations also. But this is not routine.

a friendly atmosphere. The emotional bond so tunes up their bodies that their menstrual cycles synchronize†. It almost means a communion in consciousness. But how is the communication between these separate units of bodily existence established? And if hormones are responsible for the menstruation, then who modulates the hormones? There is no answer in our scientific paradigm. But if we were to recognize that consciousness may have a wave-like function and "body-mind" may give out such waves of consciousness that superimpose and synchronize, this is explained.

Bruce Effect is a step ahead. It is documented only in mice so far but some of our unpublished data from humans point to the fact that it is operative in humans too. The documentation in mice is as follows: A female mouse gets pregnant by a particular male mouse. But if she were to have sexual contact with another male, the embryo may get dissolved or aborted. But in a situation where she is isolated from other male mice and cohabits with the male parent of the embryo, the pregnancy goes to term. This is unexplainable on any count within the scientific paradigm.

9. *Reincarnation*

While we embark on this highly controversial area, most of the scientists at the beginning only would deny its acceptance. But, there is sufficient data in this area also to warrant a discussion.

There are several publications on the subject. Martin Wilson[39] elaborates that Buddhist training can impart a facility for recall of past life. He also advocates recall under hypnotic regression. Helen Wambach[40,41] cultivated a special technique for reliving past lives under hypnosis and working with a group of 50 or more people, collected 1088 such reports. Francis Story[42] derives inspiration from Hinayana tradition while working in Sri Lanka. His validation comes from the ability to perform intricate dances that could not have been learnt in the present life but were a part of the life of previous incarnation. Edith Fiore[43] found that people with phobias and sexual problems, when taken to their past life,

† Some people loosely ascribe this effect to the liberation of faintly smelly substances from the human body. This is applicable to the lower species and insects. Smelly substances from such species are called pheromes and they are not found to occur in humans.

show a high percentage of violent deaths in their past life. Lily John[44] after acquiring the power to recall past life wonders whether it matters at all. Geoffrey Barborka gives the account of spiritual incarnations, tulkus, through his biographical work, H.P. Blavatsky, Tibet and Tulku[45]. Though the book cannot be said to be scientific, it espouses the cause for reincarnation through logical positivism. Several biographies of the Dalai Lama do the same.

We shall discuss in detail the data presented by Ian Stevenson [46,47,48,49,50,51] who has published by far the most voluminous literature on the subject. Stevenson is a medical scientist. He has spent a major part of his academic life investigating and analyzing the data published or provided by others and his own, on reincarnation. His methods have been investigative and analytical. By 1974, he had compiled an international census of 600 cases. One-third belonged to his own data, which he had personally investigated. The distribution has been cross-cultural and global. There were reports from India, Ceylon, Thailand, Burma, Turkey, Syria, Lebanon, Europe and Brazil. A few were from the USA and Canada too. There were numerous cases from Alaska.

His method of investigation has been the direct verification of data from the present and "previous life". His objections to the use of hypnosis seem to be cogent. According to him, there is a difficulty to control the subject's access to the information embodied in the "previous personality". It seems to comprise a mixture of several ingredients; subject's current personality, his expectations of what he thinks the hypnotist wants, his fantasies about what his previous life ought to have been and also the elements derived paranormally.

He considers that the following paranormal influences have to be ruled out. He says telepathy and clairvoyance— extrasensory perception—can influence the accounts of the subjects under investigation. He even considers that some disincarnate personality may influence the subject*. The children that he investigated had particularly some form of telepathic awareness or a gift of precognition about the events happening to the relatives and friends at a distance. While such critical evaluations are welcome to the scientific spirit of inquiry, if proved, they will add to the contribution to the larger thesis that we are trying to propound. That will reinforce the hypothesis that consciousness has a wave function.

---

* Such objections if they were to be true, would support ESP!

Often the main events have already occurred before Stevenson's arrival on the scene. Then he uses the methods of historian and lawyer and psychical research. He lays great emphasis on the speaking of a language or display of a skill that could not have been learnt. And he finds this most relevant to the cases occurring in children. Such children claim continuity of their personality with that of another person who is dead before the birth of the person under study. In contrast to the cases of multiple personalities, here the person experiences the "previous" self as continuous with his present personality. There is no substitution.

The great merit of Stevenson's studies is his scientific approach. He lists the possibilities of errors as, (i) Translation and possible errors of interpreters, (ii) Errors in the method of recording. (iii) Often there is no private interview. Often he has relied on the taped interviews. But, he has been cautious all throughout about the fraud. He also discounts the possibility of crypto-amnesia. That means that child somehow would have known a person or other source having the information he later "remembered" about the alleged previous family. In other words, an actual contact has been made but is later forgotten and only information is remembered.

After extensive investigations by a single member team, which is so extensive that it appears almost unlikely that anyone will in future be able to undertake such a vast study without extensive infrastructure, Stevenson's claim is modest. He titles his studies as suggestive of reincarnation. There is no definite affirmation.

As a counterpoint, the Tibetan Buddhist edifice is built on the rock of the belief in reincarnation. There are three main sects to the Buddhism in Tibet. The Dalai Lama, the Panchen Lama and the Karmapa Lama are the respective heads of each sect. Reincarnation is a vital belief to Tibetan Buddhism and so, all the three high Lamas have been reincarnating at their will*. But at the moment, there are two separate incarnations† of the Panchen Lama and the Karmapa Lama! The Chinese version and the Dalai Lama's affirmation differ.

---

* As the latest fiat from the authorities that govern this land goes, the reincarnations have to have the approval and "sanctity" from the authorities!

† The contradictions are baffling. But Tibet has undergone cultural convulsion through the trampling of its civilization. This is disturbing and we shall not dwell on the political plundering of this pious land in this thesis.

In Tibetan tradition, there are several tulkus; incarnations that have occurred at will. So are several Rinpoches, who are supposed to be aware of their previous births. Juxtaposed with the rational, didactic and materialistic approach, how will these beliefs stand? The Dalai Lama answers the question simply by saying that it is for the Tibetan people whether they would search for his reincarnation. Regardless, he says, he would continue to seek rebirth as long as the miseries of the people last!

10. Transference and Charisma

There develops a feeling of being specially connected between two or more people in the course of their interaction. This is most commonly seen in the therapeutic situations between the physician/therapist and the patient/client. It grows and converts into dependence. This is labeled as transference.

And the charisma is widely known and experienced. The leaders of the mankind have time and again exhibited this quality so that they may command a vast majority of people to follow them and willingly sacrifice for the causes espoused by them. Buddha, Moses, Jesus, Confucius, Socrates, and Mohammed are known to all as such charismatic leaders. But they are not confined to distant history only. Mahatma Gandhi, Marx, Mao Tse-tung, Abraham Lincoln, Franklin Roosevelt, Martin Luther King and Kennedy brothers belong to the last century only. The influence of the last few names is not only love inspiring: it is awe inspiring so that even the political scientist that John Gailbraith is, was made to exclaim that their occurrence is extraordinary[52]. He further elaborates:

> Once the belief is won, whether by explicit or implicit conditioning, the resulting subordination to the will of the others…follows. Such leaders owed little or nothing to their physical strength or their personal resort to codign power. Less evident qualities accorded them the ability to bend millions or hundreds of millions durably to their will. So, of course, more than just personality was required.

What is that which is more than just "personality"? We believe a large/massive quantum electro-dynamic field around such persons explains the phenomena of transference and charisma.

11. *Déjà vu Phenomenon*

Most people have experienced a feeling, coming all of a sudden, without any clue what so ever, that they have already experienced before, what is happening to them at that given moment. This is *Déjà vu* (already seen) phenomenon.

It is not explained easily and most people brush it aside. But if space-time-consciousness were to be a field in the form of an additional dimension, the distinction between past, present and future would disappear. This becomes more evident by exploring the nature of the present. If we were to ask the question, what is present, it cannot be answered as 0 time at any given moment. A moment is quantifiable in time. Then, Gardner Murphy*[53] argues, should it not be possible to stretch that moment both forward and backward? Putting it differently, movement in the space-time-consciousness dimension would explain *déjà vu*.

12. *Paranormal Healing*

Amongst several paranormal occurrences, this is one of the most fascinating. It is indeed different from Placebo† effect. The Placebo effect is confined mainly to the symptomatic relief of pain, headaches etc. There are isolated reports that supposed discovery of a new cancer curing drug and its administration has led to remission of the disease: only to relapse when the drug was reported to be ineffective. Paranormal healing would amount to a miracle for most of the people. However, modern understanding of the mind-body as a single entity can partly explain some of the cases on the basis of cascade of molecular biological events arising from faith.

Before we proceed to explain this as communion of consciousness, let us see at least a few instances about which we

---

* Gardner Murphy has the distinction of being the President of The Society for Psychical Research in Britain as well as USA.

† More than 50 per cent of the subjects, when given powdered chalk, show at least 50 per cent of relief in their symptom like headache in a double blind trial. In this model of standard research, the subject under study does not know that he has not been given real drug. This is due to the natural healing response that comes about from the belief that the correct treatment is being given. The body responds by starting the chain of molecular biological events that are part of the healing process. The phenomenon is called placebo response.

have firsthand knowledge*. The instances concern renowned sage, J. Krishnamurthy. Fraud is out of question here. J. Krishnamurthy said that *amma* (this is how he used to refer to Annie Besant) told him that his hands had healing powers. Out of compassion, he would offer such healing to people who approached him for help. We have known three such persons personally.

1. A live illustration is a spiritual lady, Vimla Thakar. She is now in her eighties. We have known her through her discourses and books for last three decades. But, in March 2003, we made a journey (the word pilgrimage would be more appropriate) to her residence at Mt. Abu to know the matter personally from her. She confirmed that, following very arduous toils during *bhoodan* movement, she had a middle ear infection that was resistant to the drugs and surgery. Krishnamurty gave her a few healing sessions. The discharge was totally gone. The cure was confirmed at Bombay and London. The ear is well even today.

2. Rohit Mehta was a freedom fighter who was imprisoned by the British five times. At the fifth confinement to jail in nineteen thirties, he suffered from hemiplegia. He was discharged on parole and admitted to a hospital in Bombay and was dying. We have the account of his recovery in his own words since we have personally known him for two decades before his death. To quote him in his own words[54]:

> In my last imprisonment I became seriously ill. At the insistence of Mahatma Gandhi I agreed to be released on parole. Gandhiji had arranged for my hospitalization in the K.E.M. Hospital to be treated by the best doctors of the time. I was in bed for eighteen months with spinal paralysis and doctors gave up all hopes of my recovery. One of the well-known figures in India's political struggle, Mr. Jamanadas Dwarkadas, used to visit me in the hospital. One day he asked me: "May I persuade Krishnaji to come here to see you?" I, of course, told him that I would be immensely pleased if he could come. The next day I saw Krishanji in my hospital ward along with Mr. Jamanadas Dwarkadas. Krishnaji was near my bed for more than an hour and a half. I could not sit up and so I had to remain lying down. Krishnaji and I talked on many subjects.

* The instances do not fulfill the criteria of a controlled scientific experiment.

> While getting up to go, he asked me what my trouble was and what the opinion of the doctors was. I told him that the doctors had diagnosed my illness as spinal paralysis. Krishnaji touched my spine with his fingers for a minute or two and went away. But such was the marvelous effect of his touch that within a week I was able to sit up in bed and within two months I could walk and after some time I was completely restored to my normal health. The doctors attending on me were astonished to see my recovery and told me that my cure was not due to their treatment. They said that they did not know how I was cured and that they had not known so complete a recovery from spinal paralysis in medical history. There is no doubt that my recovery was due to the miracle of Krishnaji's touch.

3. This is about a British gentleman whom we came to know for a short while at the Theosophical Society at Adyar, Chennai about a decade ago. He narrated two instances in his own family. One of his sons had leukemia (blood cancer) and Krishnamurty's healing cured him. He was alive then. The other instance was about his second son. He had cancer of kidney. He could not be cured and Krishnamurty told him to give up.

We have been deeply involved with paranormal healing. Being scientists ourselves, even when we are convinced that a phenomenon does happen in nature, we insist on knowing how. Rajni asked Rohit Mehta persistently to explain and he wrote back:

March 16th, 1986
My Dear Rajni,

Thank you very much for writing to us, seeking clarifications about certain matters that we had discussed. I wish we had more sittings together. The matters that you have raised need to be discussed rather than dealt with in a letter. But there are two things that need to be born in mind:

1. The whole image therapy is in an experimental stage. No clear-cut method, therefore, can be indicated. The experiment has to go on for some time all over the world before anything positive can emerge. Here the experiments must be both by medical people as also by lay people.

2. It has to be remembered that we are dealing with human beings and not with machines. No static approach will ever do and all the methods have to be very tentative. Each human being is unique and, therefore, his problems and situations are also unique. They cannot be put in the framework of the average. Each human case has to be approached anew each time.

Bearing this in mind, we have to explore a threefold approach or method.

There has to be a self-experiment. Each medical person must experiment this approach personally first. For this he may take up some small problem in his or her own life and see whether image-treatment helps. Or he may experiment on some healthy person with reference to some comparatively small problem. If the approach of the image therapy helps, then one may vary the experiment and see whether image therapy enables the physician himself to make his self free from a particular psychological difficulty.

The physician who has thus far tested the validity of this approach can experiment on some patient not involved in any serious ailments. But for this experiment there must be a perfect rapport between the doctor and the patient. It must be a rapport between two persons, not between the patient and a professional. In this state the doctor can try the image therapy and move along in a clear and systematic manner.

The experiment on the patient must be on the following lines:

- The patient must be induced to relax with the help of soft music or chanting of mantras or may be by showing the pictures or slides of natural beauty.
- The patient must be induced to relate his life story. He must speak about incidences and experiences in his own life but not about the ailment. The life story should be narrated clearly and as far as possible chronologically.
- Taking cue from the patient's narration, the doctor can pick up some positive element about the patient's capability. The doctor can put the question along the positive lines creating within the patient a sense of confidence, making him aware of what this can do.
- The doctor can then describe to the patient varying circumstances of life, describing in as detailed a manner as

possible and watch the patient's reactions and responses. In fact the patient must be exposed to the description of circumstances and events involving people with whom the patient is related.

The patient may now be asked to lie down with closed eyes, or just be quietly relaxed, or may even dose off. It is now that the doctor can utilize the image therapy experiment as follows:

- The doctor must be in a state of complete relaxation—he must evolve his own method to relax.
- The doctor must create within himself a release of more energy. He must clearly and intensely visualize some happy moments—something, which evokes pleasure.
- He then concentrates on the patient's condition free from the particular illness. Visualize strongly and intensely that the patient is free from his illness. Actually see the patient moving about in a perfectly happy and healthy state.
- The doctor must now sit completely quiet and silent for some time releasing as it were the image of health that he had formed of the patient.

After regular experimentation for a few days, the patient may be induced to do self-healing. Here the patient can be slowly trained to the fourfold process of image therapy, viz.

- Conservation of energy-relaxation,
- Creation of new energy visualizing something immensely pleasurable,
- Concentrating this fresh energy on some spots of illness visualizing their complete cure, and
- Communication of the visualized images in complete silence.

In brief, image therapy must follow three fundamental steps: (i) Self-experimentation, (ii) Doctor's projection of healthy image on the patient, and (iii) inducing the patient himself to do the healing.

The disease process is the outcome of defeat of the immune system by the environmental forces, may be from outside or within (mind). This is true about the infective diseases as well as cancer. A new discipline that is fast developing is psycho-neuro-immunology.

It traces the effects of psychological events on the nervous system and subsequent transfer to immune system. The cure as in case of Vimla Thakar having an intractable infection can arise by immune enhancement. The cancer regression/cure as cited in the case of a British subject can also be due to immune enhancement or activation or repression of a certain gene*. The recovery of nervous deficiency is truly exceptional since there is no regeneration in nervous system. Yet it is plausible since the functioning of the brain is now established, mainly by the work of Neuro Surgeon Penfield, to be on the pattern of engram[55] and hologram[56,57]—a kind of field surrounding the localized area that is primarily responsible for a particular function.

From what is said above by Rohit Mehta as a practical guide to conduct paranormal healing, it seems probable that the therapist develops a quantum field of consciousness of both the participants—the therapist and the subject. Dora Kunz explores the various possible hypotheses for paranormal healing and has her own emphasis on the healing process being an interaction of energy fields[†*58]. There was an attempt at scientific investigation of the therapeutic effects of touch as Therapeutic Touch[59] by Dolores Krieger but the attempt did not go beyond a couple of cases.

Taking the hypothesis a step further, coherence of the quantum fields brings about not only reversal of energy depletion but also rejuvenation. This is what Deepak Chopra calls quantum healing[60,61‡†]. However, he does not make clear distinction between

---

* Only recently a gene is located that is responsible for myeloid leukemia. And it is now possible to manipulate the said gene by appropriate gene manipulation—gene therapy. What was once a lethal illness, gets cured in a few weeks' time. And the new generation of psychobiology claims to manipulate the genes through the altered states of consciousness. See ref. Rossi, E.L., *The Psychobiology of Gene Expression*, ref. No. 70.

† However, this approach is nowhere near the QED field. It is mainly derived from the Classical Indian tradition.

‡ Deepak Chopra has been labeled as a storyteller by some and some blame him for quantum hype. Quantum physics like any other branch of physics requires empirical proofs. Lacking such support, the seminal work by Prof. Amit Goswami has been stamped as "quantum babble" by some hard core scientists (John Poynton, What survives? An Essay Review of Goswami's Physics of the Soul, *J. Soc. Psy. Research.*

mind and consciousness and his usage of the word quantum is more literary than physical.

13. *Anomalous Survival: HRM Phenomenon: Prahlad Jani: David Blaine: Hibernation*

It is usual to come across people in India of most unusual kind. At present, there is one Chanduma, a middle aged lady living at Gadsisi in Kutch, Gujarat. She lives only on water. Same story applies to one Sarevshwarima, living at Svargarohan Ashram at Ambaji. And there are many more in the folklore. But we can vouchsafe for the following two—Hira Ratan Manek and Prahlad Jani. The Londoners have witnessed David Blaine and BBC has reported on him.

We met this remarkable person, Hira Ratan Manek, on 14-3-2004. He was 67 years then. He claimed that since 1995, he had not eaten any food and survived on sunlight. He used to take 1.5 liters of water daily and occasionally a cup of tea. This is hard to believe phenomenon was tested under the surveillance for 411 days at Ahmedabad by a team of 15 expert doctors in 1995 (Shah, S.V., *Prolonged fasting: How is it Possible?—A Hypothesis*, Gujarat Medical Journal, 58; 31-35, 2001). He had undergone similar investigations earlier for 200 days and 130 days. The investigations were limited to a particular number of days on the grounds of feasibility and not on his limitation to carry them onwards: meaning thereby that he did not need to eat thereafter.

When we met him, he appeared to be ordinarily a healthy man, rather young for his age. He did not talk of any mysterious ways. He is an engineer by education and a believer in science. He is well aware that one of the important proofs for any scientific experimentation is the repeatability and reproducibility. So he says anybody is free to test his method. All that one has to do is to gaze at the rising morning and setting evening sun. The exercise begins with 15 seconds and extends by 5 seconds everyday to about 45 minutes over a period of six months. After six months, the ritual of sun gazing is no longer necessary. Thereafter one has to walk on the soil for about 45 minutes everyday.

67.2; 148, 2003). Let us not forget that philosophy is the mother of all sciences.

What is the scientific explanation for his survival? Dr. Sudhir Shah hypothesizes a four-tier mechanism or anyone or more of them as follows:

1. Reducing a caloric requirement by chronic adaptation,
2. Deriving energy from cosmic sources—chiefly, solar energy,
3. Utilization of the energy in efficient way and recycle of the same in his body, and
4. Genetically or phenotypically a different body disposition.

HRM's explanation is that he imbibes solar energy through the eyes. The morning and evening sun is preferred for the gentleness of the sunbeam. The solar energy is sufficient to carry on the metabolism. After six months, the body gets converted into a kind of "solar chip" so that in addition to the eyes, it can imbibe solar energy from all over the body surface during the time of ordinary exposure to sun. The theory sounds elegant and in addition to him, there are numerous sun gazers found on the Internet as additional important empirical proofs.

(The Food of the Gods, and Mikael Alvanhor's book on *The Splendor of Tiphareth: The Yoga of Sun*). The last named book mentions a lady who had no food for six decades. However, it appears that there can be lot of chaff to be weeded out from the wheat.

There is no doubt that this man is no hoax. Two of the NASA scientists, Brenald Robert Abell and another—have taken personal interest. HRM says that they have investigated him and he was to go to the USA for further investigation. The replicability is limited in the sense that not all those who tried to follow his method have succeeded.

Since the experiment begins with the sun gazing let us pursue this route further. We have discussed photosynthesis earlier. This is a clear example of quantum event in plant kingdom. Plants are a lower order of life. This route of building complex molecules through the agency of photons may as well be available to the animal kingdom—a higher order of life. Further evidence is added by the fact that the rods in the retina contain a substance rhodopsin—alternately called visual purple—that has structure similar to chlorophyll found in green plants. To recapitulate, chlorophyll through its carbon chains and bonds, in the presence of sunlight synthesizes complex molecules for the plants. While the central structures of the two molecules are different, the carbon chains are remarkably similar. What requires to be proved, before we can exclaim, "It is elementary, my dear Watson," is that rhodopsin and events subsequent to impingement of photon upon it, can indeed, de facto, undertake photosynthesis in human beings. That the photons are involved in the perception of light at the retinal surface is elementary.

Now, rhodopsin is composed of two compounds: opsin, a protein molecule and 11-cis-retinal which is derived from Vitamin A. The photon ionizes 11-cis-retinal and in the process 11-cis-retinal converts itself into a substance called all-trans-retinal. This substance activates opsin, the protein molecule. This in turn causes activation of a G protein molecule called transducin causing further events in the internal biochemical pathway that ultimately alters the release of neurotransmitters from the synaptic region of the cell. At the synaptic junction the rod relays the information to bipolar neuron of the optic nerve where it is perceived as an electrical impulse and conveyed to the brain. The process is photo-transduction. It occurs after a photon strikes at a rod in the retina- and it is estimated that one human retina contains 130 million rods.

Phototransduction thus involves a quantum event that activates chemical ionization and protein conversion. This finally causes an electrical impulse. Dr. Shah, a neurophysician, explores the neural pathway in the retinohypothalamic tract. This is the tract along which the electrical impulse generated as per the discussion above travels, *not only to the hypothalamus but also further to the* pineal gland*. While the pineal gland's role as the regulator of circadian rhythm seems to be established, more research is needed before it is stamped as *the commander of all endocrine glands.* There is but one empirical evidence that the gland may indeed have a major role in HRM phenomenon; that is, the size of HRM's pineal gland: 8 × 11 mm-on MRI scanning against the normal size in humans which is 6 × 8 mm.

While this opens up a direction to investigate, we shall have yet to prove protein and other nutrient substance synthesis from

* While the exact function of the pineal gland is yet to be scientifically deciphered, it remains the favourite organ of the tantriks, mystics and philosophers including Rene Descartes.

the atmospheric nitrogen and carbon etc. to explain survival. That remains a tall order.

And we got the following information about Prahlad Jani (Mataji) through personal contacts with Dr. Urman Dhruv and Dr. Sudhir Shah:

23 November, 2003/March-April 2004

Association of Physicians of Ahmedabad was invited to supervise the protocol to verify the claim made by Mr. Prahlad Jani that he was not passing urine for a prolonged period and not taking anything orally including food or liquid for the same period.

Mr. Jani is a male aged 76 years claiming to reside in caves of Ambajee* near Gabbar in Gujarat, India, for many years. According to him, Mataji blessed him at the age of 8 and since then his demands for food and water disappeared and he did not require passing urine.

Association of Physicians of Ahmedabad, India, is a non-biased body made up of 20 committee members and 400 + members, all being the most reputed physicians or super specialists of the city. We decided to make a panel of doctors which included eminent physicians, cardiologists, neurologists, neurosurgeon, gastroenterologist, surgical gastroenterologist, endocrinologist, diabetologist, nephrologists, urosurgeon, ENT surgeon, psychiatrist, ophthalmologist, genetic counselor, radiologists, sonologists and many more. The secretary of the Association Dr. Urman Dhruva took overall charge. Dr. Sudhir Shah headed the panel. Sterling Hospital agreed to bear the cost and sponsor the whole project. Dr. V.N. Shah represented the hospital. Many of the committee members of our association also examined Mr. Jani and opined as follows:

Mr. Jani underwent an affidavit as suggested by the ethical committee of the hospital. He was explained all the facts of his condition and the critical points when the committee of doctors would advise him to stop the attempt or the committee would withdraw its association with him. Mr. Jani was kept in Neuro ICCU for first 24 hours and then as per the protocol decided by

---

* Ambaji is the location of the temple of a Goddess; She is supposed to be the embodiment of divine energy. There are several such locations in India and are called *"sakti-pith"*—the seat of energy.

the committee, he was shifted to a specially prepared room (no. 604) where the toilet was sealed off. Arrangement for 24 hour video camera shooting was made in the room. Round the clock security was arranged outside the room which was having a fully glass paneled door. A hospital staff was appointed on rotational basis to stay inside the room throughout 24 hours. Mr. Jani agreed to avoid bath for the first 7 days and 100 ml water was given to him daily under supervision for mouth wash and was collected back after measurement. He underwent all possible investigations at the base line of which all were normal. During the project, he underwent regular blood investigations daily or on alternate days as suggested by the team of doctors. We took serial ultrasonography of urinary bladder as many as two times a day and MRI of brain and gut. He was allowed free movement in the room and was permitted to offer prayers as per his requirement.

The attempt started on 12th of November, 2003 and the committee went on reviewing the reports daily to decide the further steps. Initially the attempt was to continue for 7 days but his health and investigations allowed us to carry on up to the 10th day. The committee kept a close watch on all his parameters. After day 10, the committee was satisfied with the following matter:

1. The protocol was strictly adhered to.
2. Mr. Jani has not passed or dribbled urine during these 10 days.
3. He has not taken anything by mouth or by any other routes—not even water for 10 days.
4. All his parameters are till date within critical range decided by the committee.
5. He has shown evidence of formation of urine, which seems to be reabsorbed from his bladder wall. However, at present the committee does not have any scientific explanation for the same but the help of senior scientists and medical personnel of the country is being taken for the same.

Actually, the laboratory of DIPAS [Defence Institute of Physiology and Allied Sciences] was involved from day 1 in this project. Professor Selwamurthy was guiding the project and the committee was in daily touch with this scientist. He had agreed to do further research. This was not an attempt to prove or disprove anyone but an effort to understand a new dimension in the medical science.

Obviously, the medical/physiological exploration of such a phenomenon would be limited to the certification that the person was genuine and was normal at the conclusion of the observation. Yet there is a remarkable difference between these experiments from the illusionists. Even when David Blaine claimed that last time he fasted for 44 days hanging from a transparent Perspex box on the Thames Bridge, there was no stunt or illusion, on termination of his fast, he was in a state of starvation. He had lost one-third of his body weight and required to be hospitalized. And during the entire period of his experiment, he lay cuddled in a sleeping bag. According to Prof. Jeremmy Powell Tuck, he needed five days before he could be restored to normal eating. (Web page BBC news, last updated 30/11/2003). HRM also had lost weight. Though Prahlad Jani and he both went through some physiological changes like reduction of the pulse rate, blood pressure and respiratory rate, they were normal human beings at the time of termination of the experiment. HRM on 401st day of the experiment climbed a hill about 1500 ft. high within one and a half hour!

There are at the present time a few people alive who get buried underground for a number of days and are dug up alive. The physiologists have investigated this and the findings suggest that the individual undergoes a metabolic shut down like the frogs that hibernate for months together. The HRM phenomenon and Prahlad Jani—Mataji incident are distinctively different in the sense that they carried out the normal activities without nutrition. The thermodynamic process of entropy is irreversible. So they must have an alternate mechanism of energy assimilation.

If the energy is derived from sunlight, the photons have supplied it. The photon being a subatomic particle, its impingement on the retina may have set up a quantum event. How does this quantum event generate energy that can cause the manufacture of proteins, carbohydrates and fats in the body? And how does it bring about generation, propagation and expansion of spiritual qualities? The question is of profound semantic significance that defies even a theoretical explanation. This, combined with the fact that not all who have had resorted to sun gazing have experienced what HRM has, points to the subjective factor and subtle esoteric practices. HRM writes to a friend:

When you gaze at the sun, you have to have a *"sankalpa"* in your mind—the short sentence that defines your wish. Also think how the sun rays are entering your *"subchakra"* called *"kalpa vriksha"* (wish fulfilling tree) right beneath *Anahata chakra.*

So the *tantra* is involved. *Tantra* translates as technique. And when you go deeper with HRM, he does mention the "subtle energy fields" like *bala, ati-bala, surya yoga* and so on. This is a far cry from the simplistic explanation of "solar energy". Moreover, a cuckoo does not make up for the spring. Even when HRM claims that about 3000 people are following his method, a large series of carefully investigated cases is needed for scientific validation.

14. Materialization of Objects and Persons

In the entire range of paranormal occurrences, this is most controversial and highly contested. The protagonists argue on naïve grounds of inter-convertibility of matter and energy as if it can be brought about in a wink of the eye. No logical proofs can be adduced whatsoever. Even the occurrence of such events is seen as most improbable and whatever "empirical data", that is there has been labeled as fraud at some time or other.

Yet, if this were to be ever true, the only material basis could be undulation of an energy field bringing about the complex form of matter as paper and ink, watches and such other articles as cup and soccer and actual human form. The narration of such anecdotes can fill volumes[62] but will hardly add value to our discussion. So we restrict the data to two such instances with which we have some personal connection.

1. Mahatma's letters are a part of sacred heritage of The Theosophical Society and are said to be written by the Mahatmas (literally translates as highly evolved souls; they are said to be ageless and formless beings. They are supposed to be guiding the activities of the Society. They would, therefore, correspond with the Bodhisattva concept of Buddhism). The letters, materializing from nowhere, were received by Madame Blavatsky and contained guidance as to how to conduct the affairs of the Society. This has caused enough turmoil in the Society. A.P. Sinnet also received similar letters and Miss Hoffman gifted these letters to the British Museum. The other letters are in the archives. Also included there is a turban left by one of the Mahatmas. Madame Blavatsky herself

is said to have materialized a cup and soccer when she took an uninvited guest to meet the British Viceroy at Simla. The guest is said to be one of the Mahatmas and there was no additional cup and soccer available as a set.

2. Vimla Thakar told the following account of the materialization of a person to us*:

> Coming out of meditation one day, she found that Thakur† was standing in front of her in the form of physically incarnate self! She was spellbound and kept watching him so. After some time, the apparition disappeared. But she found some grains of sand where the form stood. She collected those sand grains and they seemed to be the sand found on the banks of Ganga River where Thakur lived. She wondered whether she was hallucinating. She decided neither to get up from the place nor to take any food till the matter cleared up.

A recluse came over in the evening. He told her that Thakur indeed had been there to bless her and she should not be confused about it.

Rationale of the Paranormal

If the paranormal phenomena were to merit the term empirical data, then they have to be explained. Let us derive meaning from them. The phenomena of reincarnation and materialization of objects and subjects are hard to explain. Even if consciousness is proved by further empirical evidence in physical sciences to be a quantum electro-dynamic field and an additional Fifth Dimension, it will not explain how this field operates to bring about the phenomena. Should the phenomena be certain definite events in Nature, their explanation most probably lies in the direction that there is a field to the consciousness and we have to further define the nature and properties of that field.

The theory does not explain selective anesthesia. But if we

---

* The narrative that follows and the previous incidence of paranormal healing have been further confirmed personally with Vimla Thakar.

† Ramakrishna Paramhansa.

were to stretch the engram theory to suggest that the field that sustained the engram of the anaesthetized area was blocked by the field generated by the therapist (including self-therapist), a hypothesis can be advanced that will require future validation through empirical proof.

Collective consciousness and archetypes, *déjà vu* phenomenon as well as near death experiences would confirm to consciousness being a quantum electro-dynamic field theory. But this alone will not satisfy the criteria of space and time displacement as well as the storage of the field in human brain. No sooner we subscribe to the hypothesis that the quantum field is transcendental to space and time dimensions and exists as an additional dimension as space-time-consciousness field, there is no difficulty to explain these concepts.

Flash of intuition and insight generation are easy to explain by the summation of potentials of numerous QEDs that may have been built up over a period of time. However, that assumes that any number of QEDs can remain silently functional at the subconscious level of mind. Since the psychological postulates of subconscious and unconscious mind have been validated empirically, the hypothesis buttresses the current concepts. Whitten and Bruce effects as well as transference are then seen as the super-impositions of QEDs of different people. Paranormal healing is explained in the same manner.

Psycho-kinesis and poltergeist phenomenon can arise out of the energy potential of the quantum electro-dynamic field. The entire series of paranormal occurrences in the form of telepathy, precognition, *déjà vu*, clairvoyance including micro-*psi* phenomenon of *anima* perception, clairaudience and such other mystic experiences of sages make a strong empirical evidence for the Fifth Dimension operating as a QED field. The events in space-time are not confined to their location or to time but are defined as occurring in space-time that does not subscribe to past, present and future. Similarly an event/observation/ thought/concept in the consciousness, is a field that not only transcends space-time but also operates as a field with infinite degrees of freedom (in quantum sense). The series of paranormal phenomena can then be explained as random movement in this additional dimension.

The discussion has brought about a metamorphosis in the concept of consciousness. It establishes that consciousness is not only a subjective experience but is a physical reality too. Instead of being explained in such euphemistic terms describing it as epi-phenomenon or self-emerging property of matter, we have arrived at the objective description of this subjective reality. To validate the hypothesis further we need:

1. Scientific data in the form of empirical proofs: To demonstrate a quantum event in a living system will need high sophistication but with the modern technology, it should be possible. In fact, Heisenberg's Uncertainty Principle and consequent thought experiments—Schrödinger's cat and the like—are the empirical data that supports the thesis. The hardcore physical proof will be in demonstration of a quantum field of consciousness and finding the particle "conscion".
2. Mathematical proofs defining the properties of the QED field of consciousness and the particle conscion.
3. A blueprint to access the field and establish connectivity to other fields. This is available in Tibetan Vajrayana practice. Patanjali's *Yoga Sutra* describes step-by-step approach to communion with universal consciousness. But that needs a few such individuals who are willing to experiment and demonstrate their ability. Some who claimed to be able to levitate have failed to demonstrate so.

This leads us to conclude that consciousness is as much a physical phenomena in the universe as gravity, electromagnetic and quantum fields. That it may indeed be a quantum field but to prove so will require further empirical proofs. The field operates as "space-time-consciousness continuum". The concept of "space-time-consciousness continuum" is referred as The Fifth Dimension.

Endnotes

1. Benson, Herbert (1980), *The Relaxation Response,* New York.
2. Nalbandov, A.V. (1970). *Reproductive Physiology,* Bombay, p. 133.
3. McConnell, R.A. (1981). *Encounters with Parapsychology,* Pittusburgh.
4. Julie Byron (1993). *Amazing Psychic Experiences of the Famous,* Lutterworth.

5. *Ibid.*, pp. 49-51.
6. R.A. McConnell (1981). *Encounters with Parapsychology*, Pittsburgh.
7. Ray, Hyman and McConnell, R.A. (1981). In: *Encounters with Parapsychology*, Pittsburgh, pp. 179.
8. Gardener Murphy (1981). In: *Encounters with Parapsychology*, ed. McConnell, Pittsburgh.
9. Henry Margenau (1981). "ESP and modern physics", In: *Encounters with Parapsychology*, ed. McConnell, Pittsburgh, pp. 119-123.
10. Pelletier, K.R. (1978). *Toward a Science of Consciousness*, New York, p. 106.
11. Hadamard, J. (1945). *The Psychology of Invention in the Mathematical Field*, Princeton.
12. Roger Penrose (1990). *The Emperor's New Mind*, London, pp. 541-47.
13. Rossi, E. and Nimmons, D. (1991). *The Twenty Minute Break: The Ultradian Healing Response*, New York.
14. Silva Jose (1980). *Mind Control*, New York.
15. Chandrasekhar, S. (1987). *Truth and Beauty, Aesthetics and Motivations in Science*, Chicago, p. 64.
16. Dirac, P.A.M. (1982). "Pretty mathematics", *Int. J. Theor. Physics*, 603-5.
17. Bhaskar Vyas and Rajni Vyas (2000). *The Collision of Culture*, Delhi, 19-23.
18. Nagendra H.R., Shirley Telles, Manjunath, N.K. and Naveen, K.V. (2003). *Measuring Consciousness Fields using a Random Event Generator*, report submitted to Defence Research and Development Organisation.
19. Roy, Dilip Kumar (1950). *Amongst the Great*, Pondicherry.
20. *Ibid.* (1945). *Miracles Still Happen*, Pondicherry.
21. Heehs, Peter (1997). *The Psychohistory Review*, 26:45-75.
22. Sass, Louis A. (1994). *The Paradoxes of Delusion*, Ithaca.
23. Catherine, C. and Kakkar, S. (1993). *La folle et le saint*, Paris.
24. Jose Silva (1977). *The Silva Mind Control Method*, New York, pp. 51-54.
25. Bhaskar Vyas and D.V. Nene (1993). *Changing Course of Brahmaputra*, Bombay, pp. 134-143.
26. Thomas Armstrong (1985). *The Radiant Child*, Wheaton, pp. 27-332.
27. *Ibid.* p. 31.
28. Rohit Mehta (1982). Yoga: *The Art of Integration, Commentaries on Patanjali's Yoga Sutras*, Third Section, Sutra 26, Adyar and London, p. 331.
29. Besant, Annie and Leadbeater, C.W. *Occult Chemistry*, Ed. By C. Jinarajdasa, 3rd Edition, Madras, India.
30. Phillips, Stephen M. (1996). Evidence of Yogic Siddhi, Anima, Remote Viewing of Subatomic Particles, Chennai.
31. Phillips, Stephen M. (1980). *Extrasensory Perception of Quarks*, Wheaton.
32. Srinivasan, M. (1996). *In Introduction to Anima*, Chennai, pp. v-vii.
33. Jinendra Varni (1987). *Jinendra Siddharth Kosha*, Part III, New Delhi, pp. 13-18.

34. Umaswati (1994). *Tathartha Sutra,* Tr. Nathalal Tatia, That which is: A Classic Jain Manual for understanding the true Nature of Reality, London, pp. 123-145.
35. Thomas Armstrong (1985). *The Radiant Child,* Wheaton, pp. 27-332.
36. The Dalai Lama (1997). *Sleeping, Dreaming and Dying* Ed. Franscisco Varela, Boston, pp. 177-216.
37. Bush, N.E. (1983). "The near death experience in children", *The Journal of Near Death Studies,* Anabiosis. 3; pp. 3-4.
38. Herbert Benson (1986). *The Relaxation Response,* Boston.
39. Martin Wilson (1987). *Rebirth and Western Buddhist,* Sommerville, p. 18.
40. Wambach Helen (1980), *Reliving Past Lives, The Evidence under Hypnosis,* London, pp. 24-5.
41. *Ibid.* (1979). *Life before Life,* New York.
42. Francis Story (1975). *Rebirth as Doctrine and Experience: Essays and Case Studies,* Kandy, Sri Lanka, pp. 185, 201-02, 213.
43. Fiore Edith (1980). *You Have Been Here Before: A Psychologist Looks at Past Lives,* London.
44. Lily John (1978). *The Centre of Cyclone,* London.
45. Barborka, G.A., H.P. Blavatsky (1986). *Tibet and Tulku,* Wheaton.
46. Ian Stevenson (1960). "The evidence for survival from claimed memories of former incarnations", Part 1, Review of Data, *Journal Amer. Soc. Psy. Research,* 54; 51-71.
47. *Ibid.* (1960). Part II, "Analysis of data and suggestions for further investigations", *Jour. Amer. Soc. Psy. Research,* 54; 95-117.
48. *Ibid.* (1975). *Ten Cases Suggestive of Reincarnation in India,* Vol. 1 Charlotteville.
49. *Ibid.* (1977). *Ten Cases Suggestive of Reincarnation in Sri Lanka,* Vol. 2, Charcotteville.
50. *Ibid.* (1980). *Twelve Cases Suggestive of Reincarnation in Lebanon and Turkey,* Vol. 3, Charcotteville.
51. *Ibid.* (1984), *Twelve cases suggestive of Reincarnation in Thailand and Burma,* Charcotteville.
52. John Kenneth Galbraith (1984). *The Anatomy of Power,* London, pp. 35-39; 171-180.
53. Gardner Murphy (1981). *Encounters with Parapsychology,* ed. McConnell, Pittsburgh.
54. Bhaskar Vyas and Bachubhai Sutaria (1988). *A Philosopher's Journey, Reflections on the Times and Values of Rohit Mehta,* Vadodara, p. 35.
55. Penfield Wilder (1970). *The Mystery of the Mind,* Princeton.
56. Karl Pribram (1971). *Languages of the Brain,* Englewood Cliffs.
57. Karl Pribram (1976). "Problems concerning the structure of consciousness", In: *Consciousness and Brain,* Ed. by Globus, G., New York.
58. Dora Kunz and Erik Pepper (1985). "Fields and their clinical

implications", In *Spiritual Aspects of the Healing Arts,* Ed. by Dora Kunz, Wheaton Ill, pp. 213-260.
59. Dolores, Krieger (1979). *Therapeutic Touch, How to Use Your Hands to Help or to Heal,* Englewood Cliffs.
60. Deepak Chopra (1990). *Quantum Healing, Exploring the Frontiers of Mind/Body Medicine,* New York, pp. 80-110.
61. Deepak Chopra (1993). *Ageless Body, Timeless Mind: A Practical Alternative to Growing Old,* New York, pp. 221-224.
62. Paramhansa Yoganand (1986). *Autobiography of a Yogi,* Bombay.

3
The Modern Scientific Approach

1. Time

We shall first examine the concept of time[1,2]. The questions to which we shall seek the answers are: Is time *a priori*, primordial, or did it come into existence as a part of the universe at its beginning? Does it progress and does it have a direction? If it does progress, is time unidirectional, as it is generally perceived? What does time reversibility mean in many equations of physics? Is it progressing in a straight line, in a curve or is the movement circular? Or is time infinite and limitless, without a beginning and without an end?

After the advent of Newtonian physics, when the dawn of the Age of Reason was nearing noontime at the onset of eighteenth century, it made scientists speculate that everything knowable in the field of physics was already known. It was celebrated thus:

> Nature and Nature's laws lay hid in night:
> God said, "Let Newton be!" and there was light.

This was in spite of the famous metaphorical, metaphysical statement of Newton (1642-1727) that he was but a child gathering pebbles on the vast seashore of knowledge. But now even at the beginning of the new millennium, there still are many paradoxes and much remains unexplained in science. Time is one such enigma.

St. Francis when asked what time is had replied thus: If you ask me that question, I should say I know not the answer. When you do not ask me, I think I know what time is. The position of physicists is similar. They work all the time, with time. And in the commonsense experience, all of us may agree that the time moves from present to future and that is irreversible. Yet, there are several propositions in the theory of physics as well as in mathematical equations where the negative value for time would hold equally true. Physicists love symmetry and they view nature as symmetrical. Symmetry implies a set of invariance of a system. Time invariance would mean that the equations with the positive (t) and negative value of time (-t) are both correct. In fact, in some exceptional conditions, when that does not happen, the violation of T symmetry is said to occur*. Does it imply that time may proceed either way, i.e. it is reversible like the running of a video-cassette in the reverse mode? If our everyday experience points to one-way dimensionality of time—a linear arrow of time, how is it that there are different mathematical-physical models of time?

Some of the greatest minds of our time have applied their intelligence in answering such questions. Yet this has not resolved the complexity of the concept of time. This can be illustrated when we deal with: (i) Newtonian mechanics; (ii) Electro-magnetic waves; (iii) at the sub-atomic level in quantum mechanics; (iv) the theories of special and general relativity. We shall also explore; (v) the parameters at the cosmic level; (vi) the field of thermodynamics; and (vii) psychological time. Though not a physicist's domain, it also flows backwards and forwards. Let us examine the evidence.

1. Newtonian Mechanics

In 1687, Newton published his laws of motion. This system of mechanics is applicable to the bodies moving at ordinary speeds, i.e. at speeds much less than that of light. It deals with the study of the matter and forces acting upon it for a given period of time. After more than 300 years, Newtonian theories remain good and sending space rockets to the moon and other planets depend upon them. The equations in this classical branch of physics are time-reversible.

When it comes to actual effects, however, let us see how even the classical physics has an element of indeterminacy about it. Suppose we have a finite accuracy and we do not know exactly where just one atom is, say to one part in a billion. Then it goes along and hits another atom and we find an even larger error in the position after the collision. Thus it gets amplified. Starting with a

---

* Paradoxical as it is, there are some phenomena where t violation occurs. They are unexplainable as of today (*vide infra*).

very tiny error, it can magnify rapidly as the collision of the billiard balls on the table.

No matter how precise, an arbitrary accuracy over a period of time makes accurate prediction impossible. And the time need not be very long like millions of years (as seen in the calculations of the age of the universe); the time goes logarithmically with the error and it turns out that in what may be considered a tiny bit of time, we lose all the information and randomness may become obvious[3].

Chaos and Nonlinear Behaviour of the Systems

Thus, even in a system that should be governed by deterministic laws, only a slight change in a few of the parameters can alter the equation drastically. The end result can vary in unpredictable and seemingly random behaviour—in a chaotic fashion. This has resulted in the development of a new branch of physics—chaos.[4, 5]

In such a system the equations that define the way the system would change with time are non-linear. They are very sensitive too, so that a small initial difference may make an enormous change to the future state of the system. This has come to be known as butter fly* effect.

Chaos is about the non-linear behaviour of a system with a number of variables over a period of time. But time itself does behave in a nonlinear manner when it comes across massive gravitational pull as we shall see later.

2. *Radio Waves*

James Clerk Maxwell (1831-1879) published his work on the electromagnetic radiation† in 1864. The radio waves are transmitted by the medium of electromagnetic radiation. Commonsense as it is,

* Initially, chaos theory was introduced to forecast the unpredictable weather conditions. It suggests that dynamic equations governing the weather are so sensitive to initial conditions that fluttering of the wings of a butterfly would result in the occurrence of a hailstorm in other part of the world. That is why, it is called *butterfly effect.*

† Electromagnetic radiation is the energy resulting from the acceleration of electric charge and the associated electric fields and magnetic fields. The energy can be regarded as waves, propagated through space, requiring no supporting medium.

radio waves travel forward in time. That obviously means that the electromagnetic waves emitted by the transmitter cannot go back to the radio station. However, Maxwell's equations, that are a set of differential equations describing the space and time dependence of the electromagnetic field hold equally true when the value of time is taken either as positive or negative. Moreover, under suitable conditions, the transmitter could absorb radiation. In a blackbody at thermal equilibrium, emission and absorption balance!

What is theoretically postulated by Maxwell's equations becomes important when we see the scale of validity for the equations. They were proposed in 1864. They have been time-tested by now. Not only that, their scope and range of application extended from the minutest to the very large systems. They are valid for the tiny scale of atoms and subatomic particles and also they hold true when applied to galaxies some million, million, million, million, and million, million times larger![6] This is indeed very elegant!

The elegance is further enhanced by the experiments of Prof. Kevin Warwick at Reading University, England since they include consciousness too. He implanted a microcomputer in his forearm in 1998. In the year 2000, he connected this computer to the Internet. This culminated in his transmitting a thought/order from his brain to his fingers to move to an artificial hand via Internet to a location in England! Robotics and artificial intelligence were so far in the computer. This connects a living system. This proves that the electrical impulses in nervous system do convert into electromagnetic waves carrying the information exactly *as it was thought/ordered/worded.* (Ref. to the books, *Wired; I, the Cyborg.*

Does this ever mean that Science movies, Terminator 1, Terminator 2, and Matrix can come alive?).

He elaborates on its simple applications like opening the house door and switching of the bed room light, an electronic chair for the handicapped persons like one that Stephan Hawking used and so on. Such actions would then occur by thought/orders only. But this turns out to be too simplistic now. His wife was to have a similar computer implanted in her arm. They had planned to see whether they could exchange emotions through their computers!

Candace Pert in 1975 began deciphering the molecules of emotions and the research in this field has defaced the mind body duality. If the electromagnetic transmission of emotions were to happen, robotics of Kevin Warwick would provide a link between electromagnetism and molecular biology. We got to hurry in our search for a unified theory (discussed later) of everything!

Warwick's experiments impinge further on the biological aspects. While conducting his experiments, mobile phone of a collaborator rang. There was a jerk on the graph of the neurological transmission that was being recorded. Of course, he did not personally *feel* anything—till he noticed the recorded jerk. Realizing that the electromagnetic fields would be causing this kind of jarring, he has stopped using mobile phone since then. But we exist in a jungle of electromagnetic fields as of today. How shall we clear this pollution?

Already there is some suspicion that repeated exposure to electromagnetic fields may cause cancer. If this were to be proved, it would be an evidence more about the link between the electromagnetic field and molecular cell biology. What happens to the daring couple after a few years of their "computerization" will be most fascinating to see.

The reversibility of the radiowaves to the source of origin may be of theoretical interest. Warwick's work open up a new possibility of sending radio waves to the brain of say, a patient of Parkinson's or Alzheimer disease; provided a computer were to be implanted in their body. Will this enhance their memory or thought processing? And what will such a thing do to a patient of Schizophrenia?

3. *Quantum Mechanics*

At the zenith of Newtonian era, the behaviour of nature was thought to be absolutely deterministic by the laws of physics. If we know the state at the beginning of an event, have precise quantification of the interplay of forces acting on that event, and then, it was a certainty that we shall predict the outcome at a given point of time. Putting it other way, the precise relationship of causality and change was thought to be deterministic. However, at the beginning of the twentieth century, it was observed that many phenomena at the sub-atomic level could not be explained. Quantum* theory was

* The word quantum literally means a discrete packet. During the course of Einstein's observations on what happens when light falls on a metallic object, he arrived at the concept of photon as a particle of light.

postulated in 1900-01 by Max Plank (1858-1947) since there was failure of classical mechanics and electromagnetic theory to provide that kind of a consistent explanation of subatomic phenomena.

The equations in quantum physics are time reversible. At the time when an observation is made, there is said to be a collapse of the wave function. At that point, the possibilities are said to be collapsing into one singularity. The resultant actuality after the measurement cannot be time reversed to twin or multiple possibilities. Niels Bohr (1885-1962), a founding father of the Copenhagen School of quantum mechanics, postulated that the probability of finding a subatomic event either as a wave or a particle at a particular point remains indeterminate till it is observed. In common parlance this means that a cat can be both alive and dead in an experiment as it proceeds till such time that the observation* is made. Let us examine this experiment in more detail.

Schrödinger's Cat[7]

Ervin Schrödinger (1887-1961) designed a thought experiment to illustrate the paradox. He conceptualized it thus: Suppose that there is a sealed vessel that contains a live cat. The vessel also contains a device that gets triggered by a quantum event, such as radioactive decay of a nucleus. If the quantum event occurs, cyanide is released and the cat dies. If the event does not occur, the cat lives. According to Schrödinger, the cat can be said to be either alive or dead only when the lid of the vessel is opened and the situation inside is observed. While some physicists believe that there is overemphasis on the role of the observer, the physicists belonging to the Copenhagen School [Niel Bohr (1885-1962), Werner Heisenberg

---

* What does an observation mean? If it means that there is an observer who makes the observation, this is for the first time that the role of consciousness is taken note of in physics. If the observation is what is recorded on some instrument, there is a time lag between the occurrence and the recording of the event. And the act of observation by an observer implies that a photon of radiation bounces off towards an observer so as to locate the particle. Such a bouncing of photon itself will alter the position of the particle under observation. This is Heisenberg's Uncertainty Principle (*vide infra*).

(1901-76), Wolfgang Pauli (1900-1958) and Max Born (1882-1970)] strongly supported this paradoxical proposition[8].

These physicists put it thus: there are only probabilities regarding the properties of subatomic particles. It may be a particle or a wave until such time that an observation is made. At the time of the observation the probability materializes into one single actuality.

The relevance of this discussion is that before the measurement is made, the equations in quantum physics are time reversible. It is not so after the moment of observation. The resultant actuality after the measurement cannot be time-reversed to twin or multiple probabilities.

There is no role for the observer in classical physics. The material world as governed by the laws of Newtonian physics exists regardless of an observer; inclusion or exclusion of an observer does not alter its physicality in anyway. But the quantum event involves Uncertainty Principle* and the result is determined by the observation.

What does the event of measurement, the input of observation imply here? We do not have the answer. Does the physical property of a subatomic event that may either be a particle or a wave crystallizes into actuality by the addition of an immeasurable (as of today), mass-less and yet tangible qualitative input that is consciousness? Or the observation is implied only in terms of development of the photographic film that has captured the event at the time of exposure?†

This is our first encounter with consciousness. We shall see later about the "physicality" of this qualitative property, viz. consciousness, in terms of the modifications of Schrödinger's experiment. In this model, the observation is by a series of "Schrödinger's friends". That will involve many more "units of

---

* Formulated by Heisenberg, this principle says that it is not possible to exactly know the location and the momentum of a particle. The location can only be stated as a probability in circumscribed space. This is so because in the act of the observation of a particle, the particle bounces off a photon. That affects the observed particle.

† It is also to be remembered that time measurements in quantum physics are of very, very minute order. Say, k-meson exists for 52 billionths of a second. (Ref. Gary Zukov, The dancing wu li masters. Stable particle table).

consciousness" if we were to consider each observer as a single unit of consciousness!

*The Paradox of Neutral Kaon (k-meson)**

We are now in a position to probe further regarding the behaviour of the subatomic particles armed with the understanding that these particles have properties like matter and wave both. Let us elucidate a little further.

Our understanding that the ultimate unit of the matter is an atom is proved untrue. The atom is further divided – and what a proof we have had of that at Hiroshima and Nagasaki!–Into a Nucleus that consists of one or more protons and neutrons and electron(s) that circle(s) (does it really? Or is it a field?) around them.

For every particle that is discovered, the nature has a replica of it as an antiparticle in reverse mode. The electron has as its alter-ego anti-electron (positron) and this is true for the entire range of elementary particles. Thus, we now know that proton consists of three quarks, with distinctive characters for each of them (in terms of CPT, *vide infra),* there are anti-quarks exactly corresponding to them in opposite reference. Thus quarks make up the matter in the universe and anti-quarks make up the antimatter! Moreover, if a particle and its antiparticle were to collide, they annihilate† themselves to convert into energy.

Anti-matter is no mere abstraction. It is produced by high-energy collisions in the laboratory. It is also found in the universe, though in much lesser quantity than the corresponding matter. Why should there be more matter than anti-matter in the universe? This paradoxical position is explained by another paradox. That is the paradoxical behaviour of neutral kaon.

This is explained under combination of operations designated

---

* Kaon is an elementary particle. It belongs to a class of particles called mesons. Mesons are the particles in the nucleus of the atom where they hold the protons and neutrons together. Japanese (was he a Buddhist?) physicist, Hideki Yukava (1907-1981) predicted the existence of mesons. The weight of a meson is in between (middleweight) proton and electron; it resonates with the middle way of Buddhism. It is the binding force between the proton and neutron in the nucleus.

† When a particle and its antiparticle collide, they destroy themselves releasing energy. This is called annihilation.

as C (changing particles for antiparticlest*), P (change of parity meaning reversal of sides as in a mirror image) and T (meaning reversal of the spin, as -t. If the charge on a particle is reversed, and its parity is reversed by reflecting it into a mirror, then if its spin is reversed, the result should lead us to the point from where we began. (Of course, the use of negative value for t should not be considered as reversed time: reversal of spin means only time invariance or time reversibility. The idea of the reversed time is an absurdity that is best illustrated by suggesting that a light bulb should light up before the switch is put on). This does not happen with neutral kaon since it behaves differently in reverse mode. The particle exists for a fraction of a second.[†] But the studies of its decay in bubble chambers[‡] photographs have found that the particle kaon would behave differently. Putting it differently, there is violation of time invariance.

This happens only in neutral kaon. Other elementary particles from radioactive elements such as uranium, thorium, and radon behave the same way regardless of reversal affected in CPT. So paradoxical behaviour of neutral kaon is unique. But the other particles do not do so. This is a paradox.[§]

---

* All elementary particles have their corresponding antiparticles. Their existence is predicted by relativistic quantum mechanics. The theory extends to all kind of matter. So for all matter, there should be anti-matter. Say, for hydrogen there should be anti-hydrogen; and anti-hydrogen has been created in the laboratory.

† Every Elementary Particle has a particular spin just as it has a particular charge.

‡ 52 billionth of a second! (cf. Gary Zukav, The Dancing Wu Li Masters, Stable particle table at the end of the book).

51. A bubble chamber generates tracks (like tracks of jet planes in the sky) when particles traverse the chamber. These tracks are a result of ionization that takes place in the chamber. The tracks can be captured on a photograph. They represent the trajectories of various particles involved in a reaction or decay. Knowing the curvature, orientation etc. of a track, one can identify the particles involved. Since only a charged particle can cause ionization, neutral particles involved in the process have to be determined by a process of elimination; they leave no tracks.

§ In April 2004, it was reported from Brookhaven National Laboratory in USA that the subatomic particle k-mason has its mysteries not completely revealed yet. The rare instance of its different decay

Einstein maintained that such paradoxes are due to our ignorance of the fundamental forces of nature rather than with the nature of Nature itself. Be that as it may, but, if the neutral kaon were not to behave in this paradoxical fashion, we would not be here to observe it. This is because the preponderance of matter-that we are composed of-as regards its antithesis, antimatter in the universe is attributed to this manner of behaviour of neutral kaon. It is because of this non-conformity of kaon that there are more quarks than anti-quarks in the nature. Quarks are the primary building blocks of the matter. Had neutral kaon followed the behaviour of other particles in CPT, anti-quarks would have annihilated quarks and the universe would have scarcely had any matter left and would have been filled with radiation. That would count us out! This leads to the weak anthropic cosmological principle (*vide infra*).

4. *Relativity*

Special Theory of Relativity

Special theory of relativity introduced a new concept in physics whereby the distinction between the matter and energy is obliterated. This led to the famous $E = mc_2$: thereby establishing the inter-convertibility of energy and matter*. The inter-convertibility is evident at the level of elementary particles and in the decay of radioactive elements either occurring naturally or artificially produced by bombardment with neutrons or such other particles.

And we have yet to explore the concept of time with relation to space that generates an additional dimension—four-dimensional space-time-continuum.

The commonsense view of space around us is two-dimensional. That is how the misconception that the earth is flat was current for a long time†. Three-dimensional perspective is dependent upon the

---

is found to be three times more common at Brookhaven than the Standard Model where it occurs once in 7 billion decays.

* $E = mc^2$ is mostly misunderstood. We cannot convert a proton into energy. Energy is obtained from the binding energy in the nucleus or from pair annihilation of the particles.

† Addition of a further dimension space-time has radically changed the universe-view for our civilization. There is a classic science fiction by the title, Flat Land (Abbot, World of Mathematics, Vol. 4, Ed.

binocular vision. This is a natural attribute of mankind. Yet, the acuity of this faculty differs from people to people and only a few gifted have it sharply focused like the artists, architects and tennis players. To add further dimensionality to our conceptualization of universe makes the comprehension particularly difficult. Let us make an attempt.

When an object is moved, energy is incorporated in it and its mass is increased. This may not be relevant for ordinary speeds. But as the speed approaches near the speed of light, its significance becomes clear. An object that is moving at 90 per cent the speed of light will have its mass doubled. But, if an object were to travel at the speed of light, its mass will become infinite. This is impossible: then it would require infinite energy to propel at that speed. This brings us to the conclusion that only light and such other waves that have no intrinsic mass can travel at the speed of light. We intend to apply this concept of such other waves that have no intrinsic mass to consciousness. But, its discussion is deferred now.

From our restricted perspective we got to re-orient ourselves so that there may be a glimpse of the fourth dimension. While sitting on our chair, looking at the open sky, we believe ourselves to be stationary and at rest. What is the reality? Our chair is stationary on the surface of the earth: but the earth is moving at astronomical speed in the space with reference to other objects in the space. While the position of the chair on earth remains the same from now to the next second, our position *vis-à-vis* the landmarks that we may have chosen to define our location in space has changed significantly. Based on this simple explanation, it follows that if we have to exactly define the location of any particular event in space, we shall have to be specific not only about the position in space, but also about the time of observation. This will bring an additional parameter of consciousness. Putting simply, any event that takes place occurs in the dimension that we may call now space-time.

The path breaking research in the twentieth century science that has revolutionized the concept of space and time is through

---

Neumann). The characters in the novel have only two-dimensional perspective of their world and live, therefore, on a flat land. Emergence of a novel three-dimensional character in the form of a sphere throws them into wilderness trying to grasp the meaning of the new happening!

the theory of relativity. At one time, it was said that the theory is so complex that only three men in the world understood it. The implications in the life-styles are so commonly visible today that even a child who might have seen movies like Star Wars, be made to retort as to who is the third person, apart from Einstein and himself!

Einstein was a clerk in a Swiss patent office when he first* came upon the idea that our ordinary perception of space and time is inappropriate. The exact location of any event that may be occurring in the universe cannot be given in the framework of three-dimensional space with its co-ordinates of length, breadth and height. It has to be combined with an additional dimension of time. This was published as the special theory of relativity in 1905. It is based on the following:

> The speed of light in vacuum is the same in all frames of reference regardless of the speed of movement of observers.
>
> The laws of physics are the same for all observers who are moving at a constant velocity.

It has established a different way of viewing the universe as occurring in four-dimensional continuum of space-time. Newton thought that time was absolute and it flowed equally. This turned out to be a myopic vision, since it is confined to the ordinary world affairs of our world: it does not hold true for the universe. Einstein arrived at the special theory of relativity by observing that the speed of light is the same for all observers regardless of the speed at which they may be moving. This is in obvious contradiction with the classical physics. Going by the common sense experience, classical physics tells us that the speed of light should be different for the observers moving at different speeds since the speed of the moving observer and his measurement of the speed of light should add up if moving in the same direction or subtract if moving in the opposite direction. This does not happen. Something must be so happening that speed of the moving objects might be affecting the clocks measuring time.

This does indeed happen in relation of two clocks; one of which

---

* Prior to 1905, the concept of the theory of special relativity was propounded by H.A. Lorentz (1853-1928) and Henri Poincare (1854-1912).

is stationary while the other one is moving. Depending upon the velocity of the moving clock, it slows down. Putting it differently, if a single observer was to view both the clocks, they would show different time. The moving clock being slow, there will be a time dilatation there. Since space travel is now a reality this is best illustrated by twin paradox.

Twin Paradox

Say: if one of the twins were to take on a long distance cosmological journey, and return after covering astronomical distances, the age of the twins on the earth when they meet will not be the same. The clock of the twin who has gone on the space journey would have experienced time dilatation and moved slower. So that twin will be younger.

It was just before his death that Minkowski (1864-1909) in 1908 put the concept in the geometrical form through mathematics and proved that space-time are entwined so that two observers in relative motion would disagree about the time of occurrence of an event in the space. This was thus proclaimed by Minkowski[9]:

> Henceforth space by itself and time by itself are doomed to fade away into mere shadows and only a kind of union of the two will preserve an independent reality.

Minkowski's mathematical interpretation of the theory through space-time diagrams finally abolished time as straight line. Instead came into our perception now an elegant relationship of past, present and future. Special relativity in Minkowski's version vividly represented a new geometry. The most striking feature of these diagrams is that, all of the past and all of the future for each (individual) observer meet and will forever meet at one single point, now. Now of each individual observer is specifically located and will never be found in any other place, than here, where the observer is[10].

Summarizing, the time after the special theory of relativity is neither separate from nor independent of space, but is entwined with it to form space-time continuum[11].

The General Theory of Relativity

Throughout his life Einstein was in search of one single unified theory that would hold true for all branches of physics. And the special theory of relativity, while it held true for the electromagnetic theory, did not do so for gravitation.

Therefore, Einstein postulated that massive bodies exercise a gravitational pull on the space-time continuum so that it is curved.

This is in proportion to the mass of the body in its vicinity. The theory was postulated in 1915 and its empirical validation came soon after. There was a solar eclipse on May 29, 1919. By means of photographs taken, it was found that rays of light coming from the stars travel in a curvilinear fashion in gravitational fields. The starlight was deflected around the mass of sun.

Now we have come to understand that the space-time at the cosmological distances loses its straight-line nature and becomes curved or warped*. This happens because of the gravitational field effect of the large stellar bodies like sun and other stars. Because of the enormous mass, they exercise gravitational pull on space-time. This can create absurdities that contrast with our common linear perception of time.

---

* In April 2004, NASA was about to launch a satellite at the heart of which there were four ping point-sized balls of quartz. They were perfect spheres kept at the temperature of absolute zero in vacuum. Once in the space, they were to be made to spin and how the orientation of the balls changed would be observed.

Now space and time make a continuum. But a massive gravitational pull on this continuum can make it warp. This is aptly described by an allegory. It is very much like the dimple created by the heft of a bowling ball resting on a bedcover. This commonly observed distortion is due to the gravitational pull of the ball. Rotation of the ball over the bedcover (compare it to space-time continuum) should drag the bedcover time with it. If this were to happen to the space-time continuum, a massive gravitational pull should twist the fabric of space-time.

This will test Einstein's theories of relativity. If the theory holds, the mass and rotation of the earth, 397 miles below the probe, should throw the alignment of the spinning balls off kilter in subtle but measurable ways.

The warping effect has been tested before. The twisting effect called frame dragging is yet to be tested.

When such events are projected in the form of graphs, time instead of being a straight line reveals its nature to be curved. The measurements in cosmology extend over dimensions like 10^{79} and $10^{10\ 123}$*!

This leads us to a thought experiment. If the space-time continuum undergoes a curvature by massive gravitational pull of the sun, what would happen to the curvature as the gravitational pull of the massive body became more and more? Sure, there are several more massive bodies than the sun in the universe. There are black holes with very dense mass. If the curvature goes on increasing, at a particular huge mass should it not turn a full circle?

The probability becomes even more complex. The curvature of space-time mathematically leads us to either a ten dimensional to twenty-six dimensional space-time in *multiverse*† (vide infra)! It would be interesting if there were a way to look into such a kaleidoscopic picture of reality. Alas, we are deprived of such a pleasure! Confined as we are to our present day reality of a four dimensional universe, such a perception is not allowed to us since that will not be consistent with our existence as we are!

5. Cosmological Events

Here also the great minds of our times are not in agreement. The disparity is on account of large time-scales and impossibility of carrying out any experiment to prove/disprove what is a thought experiment-mathematical equations. We may not call it speculation because cosmological theories are based on elegant mathematics. However, the prediction range is over billions of years. This is compounded with the possibility that the equations may be unstable to a slight change in the starting conditions. Then, such a system behaves quite unpredictably over increasing timeframes.

Let us illustrate this by some speculation. Supposing that the density of the universe were greater by one part in a thousand billion, one second after its beginning, this would have so affected the equation that the universe would have collapsed after ten years

---

* This is an extraordinary figure. It may be really difficult to write such a number in full. That would mean 1 followed by 10123 successive zeros!

† Such dimensions are only quantum physics mathematical probability.

and there would not have been any possibility of our discussing the matter over here. Had the density been less by the same amount at the beginning, at the age of ten years, it would have been completely empty[12].

The Big Bang–Big Crunch

The Big Bang theory is widely accepted today regarding the origin of the universe. It is amusing that it followed from a paradoxical proposition of Newton. Following the discovery of laws of gravitation, it became evident that matter attracts other matter. At the cosmological level that would mean the universe can remain static as it is—not collapse by the attractive gravitational force, only if all matter was uniformly spread out over infinitely vast space. This type of proposition by Newton was accepted till Heinrich Olbers (1758-1840) described what is known as Olbers paradox[13]. Accordingly, if Newton was right, that the universe is infinite, uniform and unchanging, stars other than the sun with a star in every possible direction would illuminate the sky at night and so it would be bright at night. We do not have to prove the absurdity of the proposition. Accepting the obvious that the sky at night is not bright leads us to a different concept, viz. that of an expanding universe.

The paradox is resolved as according to "Big bang" theory, the universe is not infinite, not uniform and not unchanging. This is proved by providing indirect evidence from analysis of data of the light from distant galaxies. In 1990, the Hubble Space telescope [named after Edwin Hubble (1889-1953)] was launched. This takes the pictures of the astronomical objects. It provided the proof about the age of the universe, evidence of blackhole at the centre of a galaxy and pictures of some of the most distant galaxies and such other data.

At 0 seconds before its beginning,—yes there was no time at that time—what we can possibly know of the universe is that there was a very, very high temperature. This is a point of singularity. All the laws of physics collapse at singularity. So, there was nothing then. If there was anything before, it is absurd to ask what it was since there is no possibility of knowing. The only data we have is that the universe was infinitely small and infinitely dense. And there was a Big Bang. This was approximately some ten thousand million years ago with a range between 6×10^9 and 1.5×10^{10} years[14].

Hubble Time

Do you know your age and birth date? And if you were confused about that, how would it sound? Hubble time is the estimate of the age of the universe. But that is the situation with all of us if we consider our origins at the beginning of the universe. The time since the beginning of the universe till now is the age of universe. That is called Hubble time. And the way it varies from time to time is a good amusing example of how scientific facts get falsified and make way for better data and theories. There was one figure to it that was calculated on the basis that the universe has been expanding at a static rate since its beginning. Then it was found that there is a slowing down of the rate of expansion because of gravitational attraction between galaxies. Stephan Hawking calculated the figure given above on that basis in 1989. In the year 2000, this has changed to 2×10^{10} years! The latest estimate is 1.37×10^{10} years. When is the next change coming?

So it is that the universe began with a Big Bang. There cannot be a beginning before the beginning. Where was time, at that time is also an absurd question. There was no time before the time began with the beginning of the universe. In this concept, it may become easier to accept a commonsense sensibility about time, viz. that time is an interval between two events. This would mean that time came into existence with the Big Bang. And thereafter it is propagating itself in a linear unidirectional way ever since. But would it continue to do so indefinitely? It seems doubtful. It is so because the universe is not static and cosmological events keep on happening. Therefore, as the matter in the universe is in such a state of expansion, this happens over the four dimensional space-time. Even if we were to find visualization of four dimensional space-time model of the universe difficult, we can conceptualize that the gravity of the dense matter at some point of time will counterbalance the energy needed for the expansion of the universe. Supposing that there is much more matter—dark matter*—in the universe than what we can observe, the gravitational pull of this matter may then exceed the expanding force.

---

* The matter in the universe that cannot be observed, nor can its electromagnetic radiation be detected. There are several theories as to why it is there.

Therefore, after undergoing certain expansion, universe must experience a collapse. The collapse will continue to occur till the universe reaches a zero size once again—the point of singularity where the laws of physics will once again collapse. This is Big Bang in reverse mode. It is Big Crunch.

There is no clarity that if the universe were to finally cease expanding and start collapsing what will happen to time. In the present-day expanding universe, the time runs forward. Shall it run backwards from the moment of Big Crunch in a collapsing universe?

While the Universe undergoes Big Crunch backwards, will the time also do so? If the answer is yes, let us consider as to what that would mean. That would amount to saying that if the Big Crunch moment were to be n number of years away from today, and if the "reverse time" at the moment of beginning of the Big Crunch were to travel backwards at the same speed as the "forward time"; time, after n minus n years, the people of the retro-universe will pass us by as the people of future!

If the answer were to be, no, it will imply a separate dimensionality of time apart from the universe. That way it tears away the time from the universe and imparts a separate existence to it. It may then converge to the axiomatic postulate that time is *a priori*. And in so being, time will have an existence independent from the universe. Philosophically, it is simple to speculate that first there was time and everything else came after. But, if time was *a priori*, apart from the universe, where was it apart from the universe? And such a distinct identity apart from the universe will also mean that the car of the universe will move in the reverse gear at the moment of Big Crunch when the time moves forward.

Such were the arguments put by Stephen Hawking[15]. But later he admitted to have made a mistake when he initially said that time should run in the reverse direction at Big Crunch. Now he said that it was perfectly plausible for the time to run forward when the universe would be collapsing. Let us hope that many, many more "brilliances" (deliberately mentioned as abstract quality) like Einstein, Penrose and Hawking would be there to resolve this riddle.

But the very idea of memories of future makes so much of excitement! It even makes Stephen Hawking to think of a "killing" on the stock market! Similarly, a journey into the past sounds improbable. Yet while Hawking may or may not have dabbled in stock market speculation and the journey into the past may sound schizophrenic, there are empirical evidences of the people having visions of the future and reliving the past moments. This we shall examine later on.

Summarizing, it may be said that the beginning of the universe was with the Big Bang. At the Big Bang, a point of singularity, the universe came into existence along with all the laws of nature including time and it is expanding since then. The reverse of this is postulated theoretically as Big Crunch. But to exactly predict as to what would be happening to the universe after billions of years is so difficult that it is like the play of dice. Stephen Hawking, therefore, preferred to keep both the possibilities open: the universe may expand forever or, it may re-collapse. And he maintained—correcting what he had previously said about the time-reversibility—that regardless, the time would continue to run forward.

Thus, when we consider the beginning and the end of the universe, we do have conflicting possibilities based on theoretical speculations. It can indeed be compared to a blind man trying to locate a black cat in a closed room at night. Jayant Narlikar[16], under the title 'Behind the Veil of Cosmology' narrates a story. In the remote areas of rural India a few decades back, a motorcyclist rode over the dusty tracks at night. Nobody had seen a motorcycle in that village then. In the morning when the villagers saw the tracks in the dust, they approached the wise man in the village to find out what they were. The wise man replied that they were the marks left by a millstone that was pulled by a cat.

The story smacks of skepticism. On the other hand, Narlikar may want to express humility about his professed field of discipline as most of the eminent scientists have done. But, the pundits of astronomy are not comparable to the wise man of the village. Their theories are no idle speculations or mere hunches. They are based on elegant proofs derived from formal science of mathematics. They only lack one important proof of repeatability and reproducibility in the sense that a second Big Bang cannot be produced as empirical evidence.

However, there is immense indirect evidence. The movements and the sounds of the Schrödinger's cat may still provide a clue to find it. This is in the form of study of the interior of the sun and such other stars, studies of interstellar dust, radiowaves received from far away galaxies and the direct observations now with Hubble telescope. Narlikar's caution is valid to the extent that any scientific fact is open to falsification by improvement from additional data or by advancement of theory.

Black Holes

Let us consider one more cosmological event. Here we may consider what happens to individual stars over the course of time. We shall have to visualize the stars as large fireballs with enormous mass at huge temperatures so that they are actually turned into atomic reactors. Because a star is composed of a very dense core, the gravitational field is at play; because of heat, laws of thermodynamics are applicable and since it is a nuclear reactor, the quantum mechanics is also involved.

When a large amount of gas starts to collapse by the gravitational pull of its contained particles, it contracts. Then in the process of condensation, the particles collide with each other. At that temperature, the collision produces helium. This is a nuclear reaction like the one in the hydrogen bomb. This releases further energy and that is what makes a star shine.

The intense mass at the centre of the star then keeps pulling particles by its gravitational force towards itself. The heat produced from the nuclear reaction counterbalances this pull. It may continue till such time that nuclear fuel in the form of hydrogen and such other gases is available. For instance, our sun has enough fuel to last for about five billion years or so.

At a point in space-time, when the gravitational pull from the central core gets the better of the centrifugal nuclear forces, the star collapses towards its centre. This is the death of a star. By this time the density of mass at the central core is immense. Its gravitational force is then so great that not even a photon can escape it. Any particle or any other object coming within a certain range,-event horizon*--will be sucked into it. That means it cannot reflect any light. Therefore, it is a blackhole. Obviously it cannot be seen. But its existence can be inferred by the gravitational effects that such

* The boundary of a blackhole. It coincides with the path of light rays that just fail to escape the pull of the blackhole.

a massive body would produce in its vicinity. And at the centre of the blackhole there is a point of singularity. We have seen that at the point of singularity all laws of physics collapse. So will time.

It was thought so for all the stars, till Chandrasekhar (1910-1995) defined his equations for the maximum possible mass of a star that is prevented from collapsing under its own gravity. This is called Chandrasekhar limit. Since it is 1.4 times the mass of sun, it will not become a blackhole.

White-Holes

One of the fascinating properties of the matter is that there is generally a workable antithesis to most of its physical properties. For instance, we have seen that there is a positively charged positron and negatively charged electron. Even smaller subatomic particles like quarks that constitute proton, have anti-quarks. So much so that matter is said to have its "alter-ego" as anti-matter*! This has been produced experimentally. *(Vide supra)*

So going by the principle of symmetry in nature, Penrose (1931-) by accident happened to propose the existence of white holes as an anti-thesis to black holes. To put it in other words, if time was reversible, a white hole would be a time-reversed black hole. The fact that white holes are not yet found may point to the single direction of time. But, theoretically, at the point of singularity of a white hole, everything is possible.

However, Penrose found this intuitively absurd and modified his proposition to say that white holes do not exist. And he maintained that even if there were a possibility of the expanding universe to revert back to a state of collapsing one, at the collapse of the universe, time would continue to run in the forward direction. But Stephen Hawking has shown that there is still so much to discover. On combining quantum theory with the theory of relativity (quantum gravity), he found that blackholes, which by definition should not emit any radiation, indeed do so. And in contradiction to Penrose, he postulates that white holes do exist.

Penrose and Hawking, teacher and his illustrious student, who

---

* There are exceptions like gravity where there is only a positive pull and no repulsive anti-gravity. Graviton is hypothesized but not found and there is not even a hypothetical anti-graviton.

are the living masters of philosophy of time, are thus found not to be in agreement about the nature of time and its various implications. Let us wait some time.

6. Time and Thermodynamics

The expanding universe implies a constant cooling off. While the energy cannot be created nor can it be destroyed, there is dissipation of energy in all the energy conversions as they occur with the forward passage of time. The Laws of Thermodynamics govern this.

The First Law of Thermodynamics states that in any isolated system, its internal energy can change by the transfer of mass to or from the system, transfer of heat to or from the system or the work being done on or by the system. While the equations according to this law may be time reversible, that is only in theory. All thermodynamic processes occurring in nature are irreversible. So the entropy of a closed system increases with time (Second Law of Thermodynamics).

While the computer stores some information and builds up some information within itself, there is increase of entropy in the universe. It is obviously seen as the heating up of the system and so on. Putting it another way, entropy is a step from order to disorder. Massive entropic events caused the towers of the World Trade Centre to fall. Earthquake in Gujarat involved a massive entropic event at the sub-terrestrial level of the earth.

This caused the collapse of the buildings from a state of order to a disordered state of rubble. There is no possibility of reversal of that entropy so that the collapsed buildings will rise again or the dead people will resurrect themselves. Even the theologians will like to confine resurrection to the guardian angels.

The entropy is experienced at all levels all the times as long as the systems are not in thermodynamic equilibrium. It may as well be extended to societal and civilization level, since they are also energy systems. Prigogine tried this in his book, Order out of Chaos. Entropy at such levels would imply that a civilization that does not attend to its upkeep would breed terrorists.

Thus the Laws of Thermodynamics point towards one-way street of time. But there are also paradoxes. When the gasoline is burnt to produce a flame, it is impossible to imagine that the event can be time-reversible. The chemical energy of gasoline has turned into thermal energy and that cannot once again turn into gasoline. But all the molecules in the flame during the process of burning obey the rules of physics including time invariance. There is no resolution to this non-convergence between the laws of thermodynamics and laws of classical physics. Similarly, at the cosmological level, Hawking maintained, admitting a mistake that he had made earlier, that even when the universe would undergo Big Crunch (*vide supra*), the time would continue to run forward; even though it would imply that there was a break in the symmetry of the physical laws.

Prigogine, a musician first and physicist later, brushes away the directionality of time thus: A piece of music run backward is a different piece of music. Following the trait of Einstein and Penrose, Prigogine maintains that time is irreversible because it is hard to believe that it cannot be so. He believes that future research will establish this thus: we can say that irreversibility is and the paradoxes are the result of an approximation or lack of knowledge.

7. Psychological Time

This is the common denominator for us all. Most of us are satisfied with what is commonsense experience. It is also true that in understanding everyday experience, commonsense is the most useful tool. The common experience is that time moves forward. We are born, become adult and with the passage of time, are gone—never to return*.

But the psychological aspect is based on the subjectivity. There are other psychological states—the altered states of consciousness—when a reverse journey in time is experientially possible. The objective parameters of this state are statistically valid. The experiences/experiments on subjects are reproducible and repeatable. (However, such experiments are not quantified.) They would, therefore, qualify to be termed as scientific. It being a subjective experience, there is no quantitative measurement. Yet, mankind has wondered about precognition, prediction, and predestination since ages. The phenomena associated with extrasensory perception of the past and future, are studied to the

---

* The theory of re-incarnation is to be discussed later.

extent that they can be verified: though not explained as yet. This we shall dwell upon later.

Psychological perception of time occurs to us because of our ordinary, usual state of consciousness. This state is what is commonly experienced; state of awareness. Time awareness is also built in during sleep so that most people can get up at or around a desired time in the morning. However, the awareness of time, i.e. psychological time, at any time, is due to consciousness.

What is Consciousness?

According to the modern scientific discipline, to be aware is to be conscious. The awareness may be perceptual of the external world, or it may be self-awareness. Taking the discussion further, let us postulate what are various states of consciousness. Ordinarily, they may be said to be, awake, sleeping, and dreaming. Perception of time undergoes modification such as slowing down, running fast, going into past, and projection into future in the state of dreaming. But there is no objective validity of the events of dream state.

Hypnosis: An Altered State of Consciousness

Since time immemorial, mankind has known a different state of consciousness. This altered state of consciousness is the attribute of entire mankind but only a few are aware about it. This state is manifest in hypnosis and meditation.* The meditative state is spiritual and mystic - we shall discuss it later. But hypnotic state is widely researched through scientific tools by psychologists, physiologists and medical doctors. On account of its clinical utility, hypnosis is utilized more and more by the medical scientists, world over. Therefore, the state of hypnosis has now been widely documented. So, objective criteria are now available for scientific validation about this subjective, experiential state.

The misconceptions about hypnosis are widely prevalent. This is because of its checkered history. It made its public debut in the West with stage shows by Mesmer in the later part of

---

* It is irrelevant here to discuss the differences between these two states of altered consciousness. Both cause objectively verifiable time distortion.

eighteenth century. Abbe Faria, a scion of a high caste Brahmin family belonging to priesthood and worship in South India took hypnosis to France. But, he too resorted to stage shows inducing about 5000 persons in hypnotic trance in the early part of nineteenth century. Such stage shows, while claiming to affect various cures were motivated by demonstration of personal power. Therefore, they indeed resulted in so much myth and mysticism being associated with hypnosis. This caused fear, distaste and dislike.

Mesmer made another mistake. The age of reason had just arrived then. The philosophy of Decartes and Newtonian discoveries had established the relationship between causality and change. The whole universe was seen as a huge clock and every event was connected to some causative agent like the wheels of a clock. Going by the scientific spirit that was just dawning upon his time, Mesmer postulated that the phenomenon of hypnosis and associated cures were because of a "field" that he called Animal Magnetism. When the Charcot Commission in 1784 failed to find any such field*, the baby was thrown with the bath water. The hypnosis was discredited and the stigma still sticks in the minds of the lay people. There was enormous empirical data to suggest the existence of a hypnotic state but the misconceived rationalization caused the damage. It attached a further stigma about hypothetical imposition of one's will on the other†. It put fear and disgust in the minds of people: so much so that subsequent clarification by Abbe Faria, that hypnotic phenomena are entirely dependent upon the expectancy and co-operation of the subject; and are, therefore, in the nature of self-hypnosis, was also given a go-bye.

This background should quell the misapprehensions about hypnosis (and self-hypnosis). We now turn to further exploration of psychological time and how it oscillates in this altered state of consciousness.

---

* It is important to note that after that, there has not been any scientific investigation about the physical nature of hypnosis. One of the purposes of the present thesis is to emphasize that such an inquiry with refined modern tools is overdue.

† Nobody can be hypnotized against his/her will or be made to do actions against his/her will.

Time Displacement in Hypnosis

Displacement in time is objectively demonstrable in hypnosis. The hypnotized subject can be time-displaced as per the suggestion of the therapist. The most striking and convincing evidence comes in the form of age regression. Age regression is objectively demonstrated up to the infant age. There is a probability that it can extend further up to intrauterine state.*

This is to be differentiated from revival of the memory. The age regressed subject undergoes revivification. That means that the subject actually behaves like the individual at the regressed age. Putting it differently, the time is so reversed that a person lives in the retro-age. The objective validation of this experiential happening is obtained by expression of various life experiences; the clearest objective expression is handwriting[17] in the form of signature. What has been portrayed in Kroger's book as referred above is nothing extra-ordinary: it appears special because it is not usual perception of time. Not only the style will regress to the age being lived; the subject signs the name according to the period—like married name changing to maiden name at the appropriate time in the corresponding age. This is shown in Fig. 3.1 that depicts an experiment conducted by the authors on 11th June, 2003.

A 41 years old lady (date of birth 10. 6.62) was the volunteer. The differences in her handwriting in the form of signatures at varying ages show evidence of age regression. The date 2.2.2000 was the date of happy celebrations of sacred thread *sanskara* ceremony of her son. Isolated and lonely as she was in the absence of her late husband, she confessed that this was a landmark achievement for her. Years 1997-99 was a period of trial and tribulation because of serious psychiatric as well as near fatal illnesses in her family. While she was happy and steady in her medical practice—10.4.95—she suddenly lost her husband. The jarring can hardly be ignored. However, the interesting change is on 23.08.1984 when she signs by her maiden name. This was when she graduated and was still a maiden. As she goes further backwards in time, notice the handwriting of a school-girl (1977). And notice the change to

* This raises the question as to when the consciousness arises in an embryo. It is not of relevance to take discussion on that line over here.

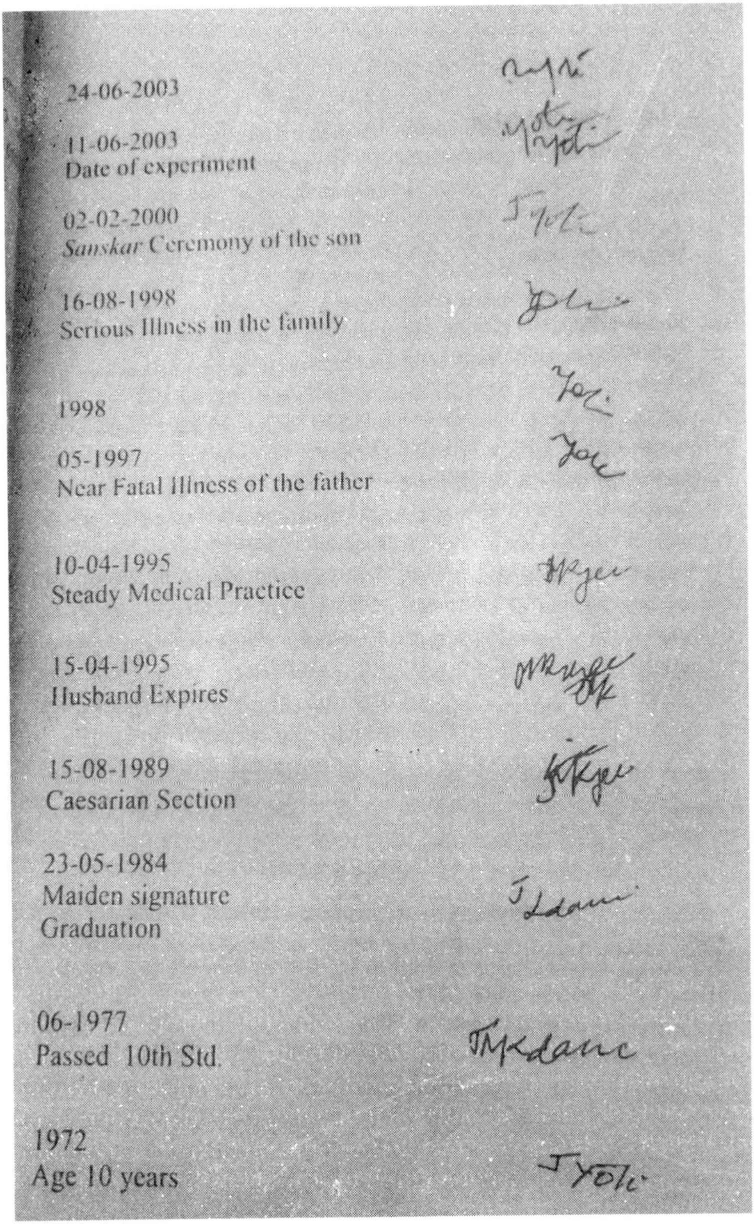

24-06-2003

11-06-2003
Date of experiment

02-02-2000
Sanskar Ceremony of the son

16-08-1998
Serious Illness in the family

1998

05-1997
Near Fatal Illness of the father

10-04-1995
Steady Medical Practice

15-04-1995
Husband Expires

15-08-1989
Caesarian Section

23-05-1984
Maiden signature
Graduation

06-1977
Passed 10th Std.

1972
Age 10 years

Fig. 3.1 (*Contd.*)

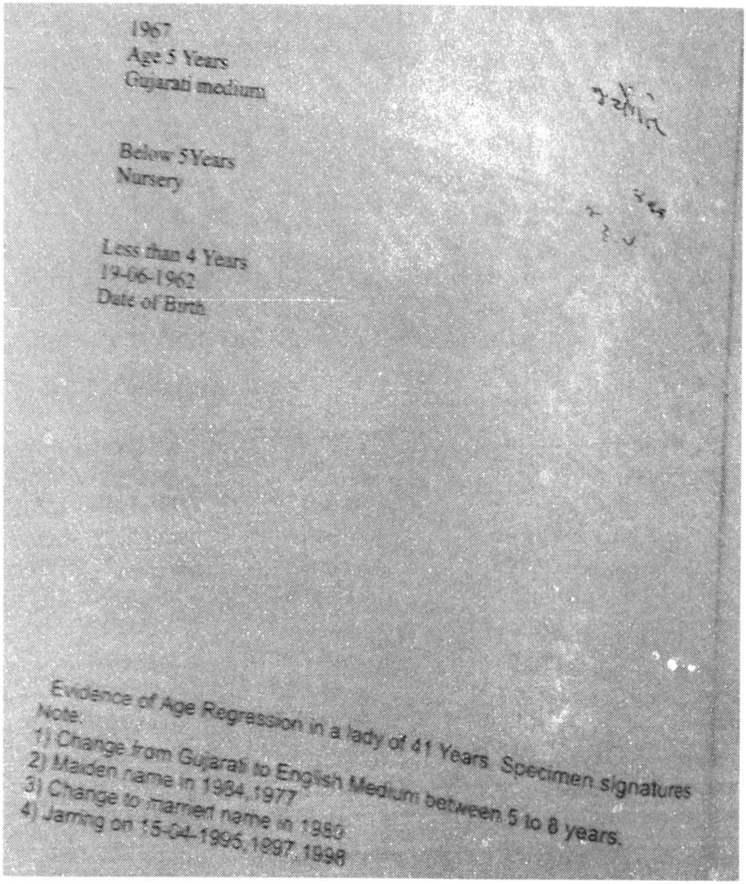

Fig. 3.1: Evidence of Age Regression

Gujarati from English (1967). This continues way down to the time of nursery school and then to the time when she has hardly learnt to write. Past that age it goes to the scribble of a child and hence not displayed here.

Further, there is selective ablation of the past. A subject undergoing revivification at a particular age forgets the period that elapsed from then. His personality, as judged by intellectualization, manner of speaking and the contents of the speech are of that particular age. Apart from the psychological validation, there is further objective evidence in the form of physiological changes. They can be illustrated as:

(i) In adult age, the normal planter reflex* is flexor (the toes move downward when the sole of the foot is scratched with a blunt object); when age-regressed to childhood in hypnosis, it becomes extensor (the toes move upwards) as is normal at that age.

(ii) A subject with good hypnotic potential (hypnotic talent) may go way up to the neonatal age, assume neonatal position and appear to be breast sucking. This is biological reversal of time.

These objective phenomena are unexplained physiologically. It is not lost sight that the bias against hypnosis is wide. The argument in favor of the evidence narrated is that scientific community in the disciplines of psychology. Physiology and medicine has found objective validation[18] of the phenomena.

This is no fantasy. For further emphasis on this point, it is pertinent to mention that University of London now awards a Master of Science degree in hypnosis, American Association of Clinical Hypnosis awards a diploma after academic examination. M.S. University, Baroda, India also does the same†.

There are several national and international professional bodies with scientists as their members who critically evaluate hypnotic phenomena and utilize them for relief/cures of various maladies.

This would help convince the prejudiced opinion that hypnosis at that stage would have undergone not only peer validation but scientific scrutiny too. To that extent, it has empirical evidence to account for in our explorations of consciousness.

Psychological Time Perception

The confusion about the nature of psychological time may be explained by a simple lack of knowledge. The brain and the nervous system are highly complex. It appears that the brain may be functioning like a computer. But there is no computer as of today, which has the capacity equivalent to brain. Moreover, the brain computes data simultaneously in contrast to the successive computation done by the computer. In ordinary course of

* The response of the toes when the sole is scratched with an object—Babinski's sign in medical terminology.
† The authors are faculty at the said course.

intellectualization, it is known that hardly 5 per cent of the brain comes to play in action. And our knowledge of the brain function does not answer the philosophical question: How is an observation made? And who is the observer?

Putting it in scientific paradigm, apart from the sensorium, which is the data collecting and recording system, how is it that the awareness about the data is cognized? To say that it is cognized through consciousness makes no difference between cognition and consciousness. Or it only means that the process of cognition is consciousness. Indeed, there is no scientific answer as to what consciousness is and how it is brought about. There is no psychological answer either and no biologist knows what the consciousness is.

The physiologists have found the brain location of consciousness in the midbrain and in the anatomical structure of those other parts of the brain that are labeled as the reticular activating system. This system is a collection of several thousands of neurons dispersed throughout *substantia nigra, amygdale, pons* and *medulla* (parts of the brain). This is precisely known. When this system is "switched on" it "lights up" the higher centers of the brain and consciousness is brought about. This we know because when there is any damage or dysfunction to these parts, the person is alive but not conscious. But how do they generate consciousness? This is not known.

The neurosurgeons, beginning from the pioneering work of Roger Sperry, have created the wonders of split brain by separating the two hemispheres of the brain. They reveal the differential functioning of the consciousness of two hemispheres. Penfield demonstrated that electrical stimulation with microelectrodes can elicit specific memories. Pribram established that the memories are stored as an engram in the brain. But how is this caused?

The molecular biologists have identified substances—dopamine for instance—that mediate consciousness. But dopamine is not conscious nor is it consciousness. Consciousness is the fundamental attribute of all living beings: it is at the root of life. Yet it eludes scientific deciphering so far. We are left with an axiomatic statement: Consciousness is. Do you need to be a scientist to know that? This is a dead end that many scientists arrive at. Many brilliant expositions by eminent scientists[19,20,21] then end into discussion of metaphysics. If one has to find a shelter in the mystical metaphysical statements, and submit to them with profound reverence, the elaborate discursive dialectics of science is of hardly any need. In any case that is not the method that this presentation is following.

The time-displacement can thus be experienced in altered state of consciousness. We do not know the precise mechanism as to how this altered state of consciousness is brought about. There is, therefore, no explanation of time-displacement or age regression in hypnosis and such other states of altered consciousness.

From the paradoxical experience of time reversal in altered state of consciousness, there is a vision of a paradigm shift. The psychological perception of time is intimately related to the second law of thermodynamics. All energy systems continuously undergo entropy and so does the physical body. We are born, become adults and die in due course since all the body processes undergo a thermodynamic change in time towards entropy. The body is indeed a thermodynamic system that is intimately connected to the psychological perception of time and both progress concurrently.

Some of the parameters of the rate of thermodynamic processes in the body are basal metabolic rate, oxygen consumption, and level of blood pressure, heart rate, level of catecholamines, cortisols and thyroid hormones in the body. The galvanic resistance of the skin is also linked with the metabolic rate in the body and it increases when the metabolism slows down—thermodynamic cooling of the system.

During last 30 years, there are numerous studies published by the institutions established by the spiritual *gurus* and independent scientific investigators that have established that in the altered state of consciousness, there is slowing down of time and therefore, concomitant slowing of the metabolic processes. Even increased longevity is claimed to occur*. Psychological time and thermodynamic processes both thus can be slowed down. What happens to the thermodynamic processes in the body in the time-reversed mode during the altered state of consciousness is yet to be researched. The studies about time flow, during the states of hypothermia and hibernation, during which metabolic rate is greatly reduced are also not reported so far.

---

* There is a Buddhist concept of *Shangri-La land.* This is the land of such spiritual masters who have mastered the technique of slowing down the time. They are said to live for 125 years and more. No such land in reality is found to exist.

Perception of Pain and Surgical Anesthesia in Altered States of Consciousness

Larry Dossey stumbled across a patient who thought he was hexed and was on his way to wither away to death. All his tests were normal but he was constantly losing ground till Dossey and his friend, deviating from the classical medical practices, "de-hexed" him. The patient started recovering from the next day and was soon discharged well. This brought about a paradigm shift in Dossey's understanding of health and diseases and it lead to a classic exposition of relation of space, time and state of health in the book, *Space, Time & Medicine*. And he found that time is an important factor that contributes to ill health [22]. If health is a state of order and ill health a state of disorder, then in the later the rate of entropy will be time dependent. If there was a way of slowing down the time, the entropy will slow down and the recuperative work done by the system can restore health. Dossey does not mention the altered state of consciousness but describes one of his patients experiencing a visualization technique while he underwent biofeedback therapy. The patient could control and cure his headaches by watching the flow of river as flow of time and making it slow down*. This process produced entirely different perception of time and abolished its linear flowing character.

This made Dossey to arrive at a formula that bears the relation of time to pain[23]. He gives the formula as follows:

$$P = k\,(S/t)$$

Where the amount of pain experienced is equal to some constant (k) multiplied by the actual degree of noxious stimulus (S) that causes pain that may be acting over the perceived time (t). There are ill-defined parameters in the equation but what it conveys as the essence is that the pain perception corresponds with flow of time. If psychological time were to slow down, pain will diminish. During all the altered states of consciousness, like hypnosis, meditation, autogenic therapy and progressive relaxation technique, the psychological time slows down and so does pain.

An extended version comes about in producing surgical

* This is replicated by us several times.

anesthesia by anyone of the above experiences (we deliberately do not use the word "procedures"; these are experiential states). It is known that sages and saints in India could bear severe pain. There are notable examples of Ramakrishna Paramhansa, Raman Maharshi and J. Krishnamurty. Raman Maharshi underwent cancer surgery on his arm without any anesthesia. But this would be only anecdotal if it cannot be repeated. Scientific stuff lies here in the fact that anesthesia can be brought about by a hypnotherapist*.

Consciousness, Universe and Anthropic Principles

There is an attempt at some reconciliation by incorporating anthropological principles that take consciousness into account. The cosmologists are putting this mathematically as the weak anthropological principle.

Weak Anthropic Principle[24]

The weak anthropic principle (WAP) is postulated thus:

The observed values of all physical and cosmological quantities (say, time as a quantity that is under discussion); are not equally probable but they take on values restricted by the requirement that there exist sites where carbon based life can evolve and by requirement that the Universe be old enough for it to have already done so.

Putting it simply, it may be said that the laws governing the universe have to be compatible with our existence. Should there indeed be time reversal say, at the Big Crunch; the conditions in the contracting phase of the universe will not be such as to be compatible with our existence.

How much does this argument help us? It says that though the laws of physics may be stating otherwise, there have to be human beings who can survive so that they are conscious to be able to ask such questions. We have, therefore, to take into account the thermodynamics and its entropic principle as absolute: since the human survival (consciousness) is dependent on the forward

* Its use is not warranted because of availability of sophisticated drugs for anesthesia. The skill is not frequent and so it is not dependable for operations.

movement of entropy in an expanding universe. If and when the universe undergoes Big Crunch, it will mean reversal of entropy; the human survival will be impossible. Therefore, the time has to keep moving forward. This is trying to prove the point by using *reduction at absurdum*. The contradiction is: this is not logical positivism. However, the anthropic principle derives its strength from its mathematical foundation. It has been further extended, albeit speculatively, as participatory anthropic principle (PAP) by Wheeler and expounded by Barrow and Tippler thus:

> Observers are necessary to bring the Universe into being.

And cosmologists take these principles further to state the final anthropic principle (FAP) as follows:

> Intelligent information processing must come into existence in the universe, and once it comes to existence, it will never die out. It may as well be said alternatively, that the laws governing the universe exist because we are here to observe them.

Incorporation of an intelligent information-processing unit that we may call consciousness, in WAP, leads to the multiple universe interpretation[25, 26, 27] in the equations of quantum physics. This is one of the interesting absurdities generated by the probabilistic equations*. Our information about the beginning of the universe is based on quantum theory. Quantum theory can give us a cat that can be alive or dead at the same time. Based on the same probabilistic chances, the theory also provides us multiple universes-multiverses! (Fig. 3.2). If we take the equations concerning the beginning of the universe, if the wave function is split, it corresponds to the splitting of the universe into multiple copies. This is on account of different alternative wave functions that result from the reduction. If one would like to take this probability further, then every component of the previous wave function is also supposed to split with the splitting of the equation that the universe was. So

---

* "Multiple universes are a great hoax. There is by definition only one universe. If I pluck an apple from a tree, it could be big or small. Do we say the universe splits when I pick an apple?' George Sudershan.

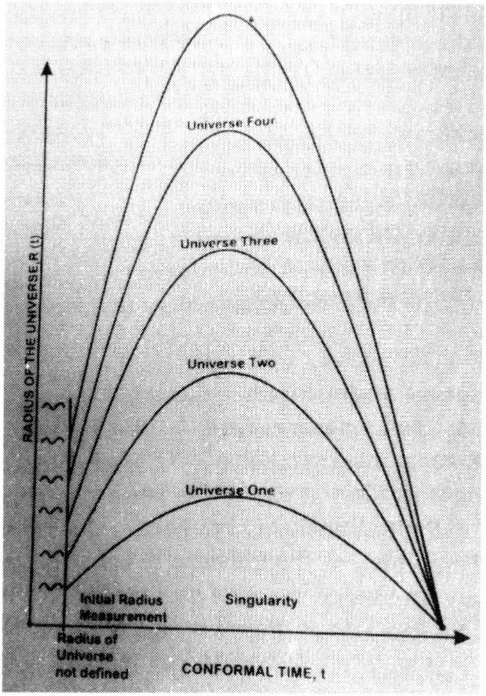

Fig. 3.2: Quantum Physics Interpretation of *multiverses*

each one of us should also split into multiple "existences" living our lives in separate universes and the absurdities* can go on. It appears utmost non-sense. We would rather accept the role of consciousness that once it comes into play, the quantum universes probabilities collapse into one single universe.

But the personal preference should have little to do in the matter of physics. Yet physicists too have their own hunches. This was evident in the famous debate between Einstein and Niels Bohr seventy years ago. Einstein had exclaimed his famous exasperation that God does not play dice. Einstein meant that there should exist something like a real world, not represented by a wave function only. A similar debate was held in 1994, between the two legends of this era, Stephen Hawking and Roger Penrose[28]. Discussing

* The word "absurdities" is used because it is difficult to conceptualize that, multiverses and our multiple selves in them may exist.

such absurd probabilities like the simultaneously dead and live cat and multiple universes, the debate ended with the conclusion that even the absurdities, when arrived at scientifically, added to the knowledge base. Physicists though vary in their opinions of the extensions of the anthropic principles, respect the WAP.

The anthropic principles not only account for the carbon particle based life, it does elucidate a bit further on the element—or shall we call it the essence—that is fundamental to the higher forms of life. We propose the definition to extend further to consciousness in the human beings (not to get bogged down with the considerations of animal consciousness, we shall keep the mouse of Einstein* as well as the clone of the sheep, Dolly, out of this discussion). The particular relevance of these principles is that they appear as a bridge between physics, mathematics and biology. At long last, the hard-core material sciences have taken the note of intelligent information processing unit, though shirking to call it consciousness. Leaving the mathematical considerations apart, Barrow and Tippler[29] elucidate the extension of the principles as:

> The universe must have those properties that allow life to develop within it at some stage in its history.

They call it strong anthropic principle. Almost reverting to the classical Design Arguments (they deny the arguments very forcefully and scientifically in their book), that invoked some form of a Creator who created the world with a definite purpose, they derive the following from the above:

> There exists one possible Universe 'designed' with the goal of generating and sustaining the 'observers'.

This is metaphysical observation that does not lead to any proof or disproof! It is almost teleological. But, when quantum mechanics is incorporated with this metaphysical statement, we are led to the startling probability as the existence of multiple universes[26].

* Einstein: I cannot believe that...a mouse could bring about drastic changes in the Universe simply by looking at it. Everett: It is not so much the system, which is affected by an observation as the observer... the mouse does not affect the Universe—only the mouse is affected.

We arrive at such a premise with mathematical deduction that an ensemble of other universes is necessary for the existence of our one single universe!*

Other explanations are also interesting. Barrow and Tippler[30] resolve it by a simple manipulation of grammar. They make the distinction between the measuring parameters by simply calling that system as universe in contradiction to the Universe, which refers to the totality of everything in existence. If such recourse to semantics were to solve our problems, every one of us would qualify to be a real savant. Even when following such diction, we should not lose sight of the fact that it is only a way of showing differences between the hypothetical possibility according to quantum physics and conceptual version of the Universe as one that is all encompassing.

H.G. Wells wrote a science fiction, Time Machine, dwelling on the possible fantasy of two-way travel dimensions of time. But can there be any real possibility of projecting one's consciousness into future? There have been movies too, like Back to the Future, dwelling upon the fantastic possibility of two-way travel of time. Even watching such a movie is mind-boggling. It may be enough of experience for one to accept the commonsense psychological perception of time and agree with Penrose that it may otherwise be absurd.

Let us conclude our discussion about time and see how it enables us to answer the questions that we raised in the beginning as:

1. *Is time a priori, primordial or it come into existence as a part of the universe at its beginning?*

The physicist's view of time is that it is an interval between two events. We are in a position to calculate a primary reality in the form

---

* Cf. with the fundamental concept of *karma,* in Buddhism, which links causality and change as intricately intertwined as in classical physics, the Dalai Lama says that there are many other world-systems, infinite worlds, and people making *karma* there. Living across these worlds, the consciousness and the subtle mind manifests as *yesterday's I, today's I and tomorrow's I,* as one continuous process. Jainism also has many other worlds' interpretation of the Universe. The system of philosophy is known as *anekantvad.*

of Big Bang. There is no way that we can know what was before Big Bang. So time began with the Big Bang with the beginning of the Universe.

2. Does it progress and does it have a direction? If it does progress, is time unidirectional as it is generally perceived or is it reversible as in many equations of physics?

Considered as a gap between two events, time has a linear progression. The cosmology, thermodynamics and anthropic principles indicate its singular forward direction. However, the paradox about the behaviour of Neutral Kaon in time symmetry (t) affirms the anthropic principles. There would have been no matter and no life if Neutral Kaon were not to behave this paradoxical way! Psychological reversal of time is empirical reality: that leads to other questions. They cannot be answered by the modern scientific paradigm.

3. Is it progressing in a straight line, in a curve or is the movement circular? Or is time infinite and limitless, without a beginning and an end?

The perception of time progression as a straight line is only a Newtonian reality. The universal time is different. It combines with space to form a fourth dimension of space-time continuum. Near massive bodies with large gravitational pull, the space-time continuum does undergo a curvature so that the events in space-time appear at different locations than where they actually may be.

It appears that the time will not end even when the universe starts collapsing towards the Big Crunch, it shall continue to run forward. But at the point of singularity of Big Crunch, everything, including time must end.

Journey through the time dimension has almost been like a roller coaster ride. It has brought us face to face with many uncertainties, paradoxes and probabilities. Shall this be our gateway to a transcendent dimension? A dimension that is holistic as it comes to unification of variables, in the sense that it equates with the idealistic proposition of a grand unified field theory—consilience as Edward Wilson puts it[31]? Apart from Einstein, most scientists and philosophers since antiquity have craved for one single theory on the assertion that the world is orderly and should be explained by a small number of natural laws. Einstein grappled with the idea to find a single all encompassing system—parsimonious, i.e. close, self-centered-system, space with time and motion, gravity with electromagnetism and cosmology. Not only did it elude him; we are still looking for it. It still seems elusive to find one umbrella for all the theories that appear to be working all right independently of each other. Unification may possibly come by combining not only physical theories under one umbrella but through the umbrella being biological science and the medium being consciousness.

If a single cell organism were to have the human intelligence and if it were to study the world, what would its worldview be? It is poetically said that a moth cannot fathom the mysteries of stars. A grain of sand cannot measure the depths of the sea. But the present-day knowledge—and the absence of it—about the quantum physics, cosmos, astronomy and consciousness (*vide infra*) point to diverse views about the nature of time.

2. Space

Space-time has now dislocated us from the fixed idea of absolute space. We all the time exist in space; but even without any movement, we are not at the same space-time location. This brings the vision of a vast expanse of limitless space, where together with stellar bodies, galaxies and the like, we are dancing—, a finely coordinated performance—, the steps, which we have never consciously known. This is the symbolic image of Nataraj or the abstract pervasiveness of *tao*. But we shall avoid dwelling further on the metaphors and the isomorphism of the physical phenomena with metaphysical concepts for the moment.

Having deciphered the fourth dimension, we are confronted with further questions: what is space? What are its boundaries? What is the space beyond them? As long as we had the flat earth notion of our world, the edge of our world was the flat boundary of the earth beyond which one was likely to "fall off" from the planet. With the present day understanding about the space, we understand now that beyond the gravitational pull of the earth, floating in the space, one may "fall" off from the position of orbit and encircle the earth without touching it.

In cosmological perspective, so long as the universe will undergo expansion, the stars and galaxies will go on increasing the distance between them: the space will expand, till such time that it may experience Big Crunch. Then the stars will cool down, ultimately to become the size of a small bean. The density of the mass will have increased that far.

At the micro level, we have equally interesting situation too. The mass in any atom is only miniscule. The atom is essentially hollow: most of it is filled with space. The electrons encircle the central proton at high speeds and such rapid motion makes an atom appear as a solid mass. Thus, our perception of gas, fluid and solid is only perceptual depending upon the density of the molecules of the substances of a given type. But essentially, whatever may be the state, all gases, fluids and solids are filled with space: just empty space.

Emptiness of space would mean that it is occupied by nothing: that is what we call vacuum. But here also there are different versions of classical physics and quantum physics and cosmology. Perfect vacuum, as per the classical physics, is only a theoretical possibility: it is not possible to obtain in a laboratory. However, the vacuum in the sense of classical physics and the quantum empty space are not identical. Vacuum state in quantum field theory does not imply entire state of nothing. The vacuum state has zero point energy. Zero point energy is the energy that remains in a substance at absolute zero temperature. If a time varying electric current passes through the "empty space", particle pairs appear!

The atom has a large empty space within it. Quantum field theory postulates vacuum fluctuations in the empty space. This is applicable to the cosmological scale too. There is very little mass in the universe and rest of its huge expanse is nothing but empty space. This is how David Bohm[32] explains the concept:

> "Matter that appears to be dense, according to physics is actually made up mostly of empty space, with a few very small particles moving around like planets, and at high energy. What appears solid is practically hollow. Although the particles may be thought of as dense matter, according to relativity and quantum physics, the matter is also a condensed field of energy...these laws are not deeply understood by the physicists...a field is made up of waves of many kinds. Each wave has a certain minimum amount

> of movement, in discrete form of quanta....the energy for each wave may be just minimal, but there are many, many waves in empty space that add up to an enormous amount. With very short waves, the energy will be infinite."

This apparently philosophical discussion is based on the theorems and equations of quantum physics. And taking that theory further, at one point, it goes to enunciate that the energy in one cubic centimeter of empty space is more than what would be liberated by the disintegration of all the matter in the universe.

Einstein's equation has made the interchangeability of matter and energy. Of equal significance is the latter point. It equates matter → energy → empty space. That suggests that matter is a small ripple of a wave on the empty space.

Putting it in other form, if empty space is equal to 0, it can be arrived at many different ways, such as,

0+/–0=0
1 electron + 1 positron = 0
10 quarks + 10 anti-quarks = 0
n (xyz particles) + n (x–y–z– particles) = 0

How shall we now answer the question: is the empty space, really empty of everything*? According to what we have worked out above, it is a field of all possibilities at the quantum state. Annihilation of a single electron and positron can produce immense energy. As we have said before, passing of an electric current in the empty space causes such undulations that particle pairs appear there! So is the empty space really empty?

Two locations for a Single Particle!

There are other paradoxical situations regarding space. Space is that which can be occupied by particulate matter. A particle which is displaced should occupy identical region of space somewhere else. But this does not happen with photon in certain situations[33]. If a

---

* The question is both physical and metaphysical. That *sunyata* (literally, complete void, absolute vacuum) is the mother-field (*pratitya-samutpada)* of all eventualities is a fundamental Buddhist concept.

photon is passed through two slits, true to its spread out property, it does pass through both at once! There is a story that Newton had two cats. So that they can enter by themselves, he made two doors for two cats. There was a big one for the big cat and the small one for the little one! Here the case is radically different. If measurements are made to find out which slit the photon has passed through, at each one of the slit it will be found that the entire photon has passed through a single slit. So there are different possible ways that a photon can exist in space. Now one particle is in two places at once!

This is further exemplified thus: let us reflect/pass the photon through a glass half of which is silvered mirror and that is tilted at 45°. The half silvered mirror will reflect half of the light that impinges on it and half will pass through the transparent glass. Putting it differently, when the light impinges on this mirror, half will continue its journey through the glass while the mirrored portion will deflect the other half. With the progress of time, a single photon now described as two peaks of a wave, as the virtual version of a single photon, will continue to travel in different directions. Imagine the situation at the end of one year. The two portions of the wave function would now be in space and would be a light year distance apart. Stated differently, a single photon has found itself in two locations at once, spaced more than a light year distance apart from each other! This leads us to interesting possibilities.

Connectivity in Space: Einstein, Podolsky and Rosen Paradox[34]

We know about fields that connect material objects across space without any material connection between them. Gravitation is a classical example of one such field. The gravitational effects seem to come into force instantaneously; however, the hypothetical particle, graviton, though not found as yet, is supposed to travel at the speed of light. That will be in consonance with our axiomatic understanding that nothing can travel at the speed of light. But, there is a situation that violates this postulate and is described as Einstein, Podolsky and Rosen paradox*.

---

* Einstein has been accused of plagiarism here as in his famous theories of relativity. Schrodinger had shown earlier that multi-particle quantum system (say two particles) can be entangled EPR. It is said that it was usual for Einstein to pass on the old wine in new bottle!

Suppose we take a system consisting of two different particles, an electron and a positron as entangled particles. They are separated and they move directly in opposite directions. The spins of the electron and positron must add to zero. Now if the spin of the electron is measured in any direction, it is found that the spin of the positron is in opposite direction. Supposing the spin of the electron were to be reversed, the positron at whatever distance it may be, will reverse its spin. The two particles are somehow connected in space; whatever may be the distance separating them. The behaviour of the second particle is instantaneously influenced by the choice of measurement of the first particle and *vice versa*.

David Bohm postulated the theory of hidden variables to explain this. Accordingly, the parameters that affect the system might be really there but are not directly accessible to us. But then the hidden variables must also be able to exercise their influence on parts of the system in distant regions of space instantaneously. That implies that whatever the hidden variables are, they cause the effects through information that travels faster than the speed of light. So long as the theory of relativity holds true, this cannot happen.

When the experiment is applied to photons, the paradox becomes more explicit. Let us consider a pair of entangled photons as a system. The speed of light has to be considered since photons are moving all the time at the speed of light. Suppose that they are caused to move outwards. In such a situation neither photon has a singular property of polarization; both of them have to be in tandem. So, if the measurement is applied to one of the paired photons, it does influence the other one too. But the other photon would be travelling at the speed of light. According to the special theory of relativity, nothing can travel faster than the speed of light. Nothing can happen *instantaneously*. How does the "information" about the correlation from one photon catch up with the other one, travelling in the reverse direction? If it does, that is a violation of one of the fundamental postulates. Thus, there is non-coherence between the behaviour of a pair of photons separated in space—space-time picture of physical reality in non-local quantum

---

Bose-Einstein equations are cited as another example. It is said that the work belonged to Bose. He sent it to Einstein for comments and the latter added his name and published it.

EPR PARADOX
Instantaneous fixation of reciprocal spin
-∪Electron....spin 0....Positron∩-
Applied to entangled photons, A and B,
After one second of separation in <u>opposite</u> directions:
-∪Photon A <-....0....->Photon B ∩-
The photons are at a distance of 1,86,000 × 2 miles.
Suppose there is a change in the spin of the photon A

∪- Photon A<-....0....
Then, the change in the spin of ->Photon B-∪ travelling in the opposite direction occurs instantaneously; even though they are separated at a distance that even light cannot travel per second. This is violation of the principle of special relativity.
(After Roger Penrose and Alain Aspect)

Fig. 3.3: Connectivity in space between entangled photons

mechanical state—and the fundamental postulate that nothing can travel at a speed faster than light. Various theories of hidden variables have not solved the paradox.

Reviewing the combined discussion of space and time and the relation of matter within that frame, we realize that though our everyday perception of these realities is necessary to keep us functional in the ordinary sense, the perception is not real. Louis de Broglie gives us a startling perspective as follows:

Space and Time Cease to Possess an Absolute Nature

In space-time, everything, which for each of us constitutes the past, the present and the future, is given in a block. The entire collection of events, successive for us, which form the existence of a material particle, is represented by a line, the world line of the particle. Each observer, as his time passes, discovers, so to speak, new slices of space-time that appear to him as successive aspects of the material world, though in reality the ensemble of events constituting space-time exist prior to his knowledge of them[35].

And this leads us to the perennial philosophy since it encompasses all that exists in the universe. The mathematical explorations lead us to the stark realization that all of the future and all of the past, for each individual meet and will forever meet, at one single point, *now*. Moreover, the *now* of each individual is specifically located and will never be found in any other place, than *here* (wherever the observer is).[36]

Summary of the discussion on space leaves us whirling in the space! Let us put our logical positivism aside for a while,—or wait a minute, this also tunes in with logical positivism—and sing in praise of mystical poetry! Am I the space somewhere beyond stars or was it some space in the galaxies that happened to ripple and I was created?

3. Consciousness

Discussions about the modern scientific concepts regarding time and space are enough to cause a certain amount of muddle-headedness. What would addition of one more paradigm into the discussion bring about? Will it bring about the settlement of sediment and give a clear picture or will it add to the cloud? Let us see by incorporating the vital element, through which we see, conceptualize and verify. The consciousness! All forms of life, at least the higher forms of life are supposed to be conscious. But this raises a fundamental question: are all life forms equally conscious? If that is so, what is the difference in the consciousness of human beings and that of other forms of life*? At one point of time there

---

* There is at least one fascinating study in lower forms that is hard not to mention here. It is about the brain of salamander, which has extraordinary capacity for regeneration. Studies by Pietsch (ref. Pelletier Kenneth, *Towards a Science of Consciousness*, New York, 1978 pp. 131-32.) in salamanders show that the brain, or for that matter the entire nervous system of salamander function in holographic pattern. The mass migration of birds in winter from Siberia to warm areas with water and food resources thousands of miles away, year after year in the identical pattern connotes collective consciousness even in the birds. And there is one discussion between two Nobel Laureates that is irresistible in its elegance. Narrated by the Nobel Laureate (1983) George Wald, it is more difficult to explain.

I was once startled to hear Niels Bohr speak of the eel migration. All the eels of the Atlantic Ocean come to the same area of the Sargasso Sea, in the South Atlantic, to spawn. They have grown up in fresh water, but now, as the time for spawning approaches, the mature eels migrate to the deepest and saltiest part of the Atlantic, and there spawn, and die. The larval eels must find their way alone. It takes the American

was no evidence that the botanical systems were alive, till Jagdish Chandra Bose proved them to be so.

Accepting the fact that the brain is the material cause of the consciousness and our subjective perception depends entirely on the brain function, we have at our disposal minute details about the functioning of the brain. We have seen earlier that the areas where the consciousness seems to originate are precisely localized in the brain. But that is only at the gross level. It hardly gives us any idea about its functioning. The work of the Canadian neurosurgeons, Pribram and Penfield has shown that the memory is encoded in the brain in the form of an engram over a large area. The function is also not sharply localized: instead it is holographic. Recovery for a long period after an attack of stroke is attributed to the takeover of the function of the destroyed part by the surrounding area.

We have to understand what the brain cells and their connections, synapses do, so that consciousness originates/ resides in them.

Material Basis of Consciousness

Reverting to the material basis of consciousness, we see its source in the process of assimilating inputs of the sensorium and as they culminate into the brain there is a progression in the form of perception that expands into abstract concept formation. And there

---

eels some fifteen months to reach their shores, metamorphose, and ascend to the American rivers. It takes the European eels- a different species— about three years to get home. There is no record of the mistaken entry of a European eel into an American river or the other way round.

No one has any idea how the larval eels find their way back. Niels Bohr said this wonderful thing: "It is just because they do not know where they are going that they always do it perfectly." May be there are symbolic contents in their neuronal network which are driving them to the appropriate situations for survival.

May be this is genetically transmitted information (how would any one decode such a genetic pattern?). It would be improper to call that it is stored "in their psyche". But better adaptation for survival,—whether we see it in the form of an evolutionary design or as a teleological tool—is at the root of this migration!

After raising this question, we do not intend to deliberate on that since we want to confine our discussion to the highest form of evolved consciousness that is evident in man.

is a distinctly different faculty of self-reference. This highly complex faculty generates thoughts, ideas and creativity. The human beings have the unique faculty of intelligence by which all such mental events are stored in what we call mind.

At this stage, we need to specify our vocabulary. Different cultures have different connotations to the words mind and consciousness and quite often two are confused as the same. This raises another question: which way is the mind different from consciousness?

The Western psychological concept of the mind postulates that psyche is the faculty by which we conceptualize, validate the concepts through the dialectic process and store the ideas as memories. Freud, working at the end of nineteenth and early twentieth century, postulated three layers of the mind and called them conscious, subconscious and unconscious mind. Here there was no distinction between mind and consciousness. They connote the same psychic entity.

But even at the Western scientific and philosophical levels, there is a schism between the materialistic approach and the dualistic approach to the mind. The Western scientific approach is that the mind is the product of the processes in the brain. Just as the stomach secretes gastric juice, the mind is the product of the function of brain and it has no independent existence apart from the brain. The dualistic approach propounded by Descartes conceptualized body functioning like the interconnected wheels of a clock. Distinctively different from the body, he postulated a separate entity, mind, which was the basis of existence. He said, I think and therefore I am. His assertion of primacy of mind over body could have been very useful had it led to the progression of argument that the intelligence came first. Instead Cartesian philosophy paved the way for advancement of material sciences. But the tide had already begun to reverse.

The modern physiological advances have abolished such a duality of body and mind. Selye demonstrated the autonomic nervous system response of the body in the fight or flight mode way back in 1936 as a medical student. But now the reversal is also possible to establish in the alternative form of flow. Hormones are the secretions of ductless glands. They directly pour their products in the blood stream. All ductless glands are known to be under master control of anterior pituitary gland. The anterior pituitary gland is located at the base of the hypothalamus and is intimately connected with it with neuron pathways as well as reciprocal blood circulation. Hypothalamus is the principal coordinator of emotions and is one of the main areas of the reticular formation that "lights up" the higher centers in the brain to produce consciousness. Going by this circuit that operates through cybernetic mechanisms, hormones are intimately connected with all varieties of emotional states, metabolism and sexual arousal. During the last quarter of the last century, brain itself has been found to be secreting more than 150 molecules, information substances, directly into the blood stream and thus it qualifies to be called as the largest ductless gland in the body. Even immunity is governed by a complex molecular cyclic chain of events. These events are brought about by the small white blood corpuscles called lymphocytes that are the real harbingers of messages concerning immune status. The lymphocytes and the complex molecules that they produce and carry are modulated by the events in the mind.* The molecular biological events that occur in the thought processes have been clearly identified as composed of specific molecules and thus thought is shown to have a material basis. At this point, thus, the Cartesian duality between body and mind is collapsing. As a consequence, more and more medical scientists are veering to the concept of a single entity—body-mind. The lists of diseases that are labeled as psychosomatic are increasing.

And reverse is also true. Through alternate modalities of healing it is shown that the mind not only modulates the body but also brings it to a state of rejuvenation.[37] As a consequence, the physiological understanding has veered from the dualistic Cartesian approach, of mind separate from body, to a singular concept of "body-mind".[38]

At the moment of death, particularly when the parts of the mid-brain that are supposed to be the seat of consciousness, die, the consciousness ceases to be. The scientific concept is that there is no separate mind from the brain. According to modern scientific

---

* It will not be an exaggeration to say that panic due to the events of September 11th, 2001 would have caused depression of the immune levels of those individuals who died when exposed to anthrax subsequently. Soon enough, there will be enough medical literature illustrating increase in heart attacks and strokes following these calamities in USA.

mode, therefore, when the brain is dead there is no mind. It is like the computer software: after the computer crashes, there is no software left.

The collapse of the Cartesian duality has brought about emergence of another hard line attitude in the modern science. Acceptance of singularity of body and mind has brought about the importance of healthy mind for healthy body. But denial of anything about mind except that, which originates in the brain, has heightened the materialistic viewpoint. Therefore, most life scientists[39] like Antonio Damasio (neurologist), Larry Squire, Allan Hobson and Lewis Judd (psychiatrists), would label any such distinction as coarse mind and subtle mind as arbitrary. Not only that, even hard-core philosophers of science, like Patricia Churchland,[45,40] basing their philosophic postulates on the concrete evidence of logic, puts up a barrage of cascading questions thus:

> If it were the case that there is a consciousness independent of the brain and which can depart from the brain at the time of death, then that consciousness is supposed to carry along with it memories that the person possessed. But when the brain deteriorates and memory correspondingly deteriorates at death, or if the brain degenerates long beforehand, how does the soul nevertheless retain memories intact? How can the recorded memories in complicated brain circuits be conveyed, recorded and carried by the nonphysical soul or mind? How does the precise ultra-structural physical changes relate to nonphysical soul? How does the soul retain such memories after the death of the body? How does it work in patients with brain degeneration—Alzheimer disease, Parkinson's disease, senile dementia and so on—who do not remember events of yesterday or a few days back? Would the memories be unavailable to them now but would remain still intact in their souls so as to be available at the next birth? The physical science with its vast and yet, limited database has no answers to these very relevant questions except what Churchland herself gives: it is highly improbable. However, let us explore further.

We have then eliminated the dualism between body and mind to arrive at a single entity that is body-mind. The schism in the Western philosophic thought is thus resolved by the science. Simply said, body and mind are one: mind and consciousness are one. So, when there is no body, there is no mind and therefore there is no consciousness after body perishes.

Does this paradigm, currently in vogue with hard-core scientists and philosophers of materialism, explain all that happens in the realm of consciousness? The protagonists argue that it does, since they deny the very existence of anything else that seems to contradict, as an illusion. They would like to dispose it off as archetypal hang over of the entire human race. But, there are empirical proofs that there is a whole range of intangible events that do occur. Any paradigm shift of any dimension has to be such that it has to explain all that is called as paranormal happenings now. That range of paranormal occurrences we shall review latter. Let us focalize now on the limitations of scientific data.

Arguments like those of Patricia Churchland are based on physiological ground. This discipline has its foundations mostly on biochemistry and at refined levels on molecular biology. Each and every brain cell has an electric charge on the cell membrane which is balanced by the opposite charge on inner side. It is estimated that the electric charge carried by each cell is about 70 millivolts. An average human brain is supposed to have 10-11 numbers of neurons. For the reason of simplification, if all neurons were to either connect in series or were connected in parallel, it becomes obvious that there is considerably high electric power in the brain. In fact each cell in the brain is connected by its dendrites to several other synapses that link the cell to so many others. The rapid firing of the neurons can bring about a cascade of successive firing from other neurons. This will disturb the electrostatic field* of many neurons at once so that a tremendous electromagnetic field may be generated. We do not have much data on this electromagnetic field except what is recorded in electroencephalogram tracings. Compared to the complex functioning of the brain, EEG records only a few different types of waves, alpha, beta and delta and

* Electrostatic field is the electric field that surrounds a stationary charged body.

locates the gross areas of their origin*. The record does not convey the amplitude and the range of electromagnetic field of the electromagnetic system that a human being is. Even the refined diagnostic systems like Nuclear Magnetic Resonance (NMR scan) or positron emission tomography (PET scan) provide the images of gross state of the brain. There is no indication about the possibility of quantum events at the synaptic junctions and, if they were to occur, their subsequent contribution to the unfolding of the epiphenomenon that we call consciousness.

Information Transmission, Transcription and Transduction in the Body

We have no precise idea as to how a thought arises in the mind. The experiments conducted on the open brain of the subjects who are awake and are undergoing surgery under local anesthesia show bizarre and yet interesting data. The electrical stimulation of a given part suddenly flashes the memory of a remote event or a musical note and so on. That suggests that memory is stored in that area and could be reproduced by its stimulation. But, what would cause the stimulation in a normal situation, we do not know.

A plausible explanation is that the nervous system is in cybernetic interplay with a circuit like mind -> higher centers of the brain -> hypothalamus and anterior pituitary gland -> autonomic nervous system -> ductless glands -> specific receptors for the messenger molecules -> genes -> translation, transcription and transduction -> mind and so on. Arousal of a specific gene causes a cascade of molecular biological events leading to the formation of specific information substances that trigger a specific brain area (*vide infra*).

Work on similar lines leading to high sophistication in the realm of biochemistry led James Watson to decode the structure of double helix some 50 years ago. Thereafter there are spectacular developments in molecular biology so that the entire human genome has been mapped out in 2002.

Watson[41] categorically states:

> We see not only that the laws of chemistry are sufficient

---

* Even then, we have the evidence that there is preponderance of alpha waves in meditative states.

> for understanding protein structure, but also that they are consistent.... with all known hereditary phenomena.... Complete certainty now exists essentially amongst all biochemists that the other characteristics of living organisms.... will all be completely understood in terms of the co-coordinative interactions of small and large molecules.... It was realized that all chemical bonds, weak as well as strong, were based on *electrostatic forces* (emphasis by the authors).

Quantum Events in Nervous System

So, all that is in the field of biochemistry, is that the final word? It is not so as indicated by the ending phrase of the above quotation. For the first time now we come across a mention of physical entity in body transactions. Of course, the perception of light by the retina is a quantum event in the form of a photon interacting with the neural tissue of the retina*. The entire nervous system functions through the generation and propagation of electrical impulses. Of course, the electrical potentials will generate an electromagnetic field. And the electrical activity occurs at the synapses as well as in the neuronal cells. Though not deciphered as yet, the complex actions at the genetic levels, from the arousal of a certain gene to the message transmission and transduction by mRNA may also involve electrical activity. Thus, there is indeed a real possibility about the occurrence of quantum events at various levels. This can bring about the play of electromagnetic fields.

Synapse

A nerve cell looks like a tree under the microscope. It has a main trunk, which is axon, and several other branches that are called dendrites. The axon is the main communicating channel but the dendrites also carry the electric impulse to the sites where they may be ending. There is no direct connection of an axon or dendrites to another cell. There is a gap in between that is called a synapse.

---

* Retina is an extension of neural tissue of the brain via optic nerve. This can be viewed through ophthalmoscope.

At a gross level it may appear that the information is relayed at a synapse for onward transmission through the release of neuro-transmitter molecules. But the matter can be highly complex. In the actions that come into play at the synapses, it is quite probable that quantum events may occur.

The size of a synaptic junction is about 200 to 400 Angstroms*. When a nerve impulse arrives at the end of an axon, it is in the form of an electric impulse. It causes the release of neurotransmitter substances so as to activate the other cell. The neurotransmitter substances are much smaller in size than the synaptic cleft, yet it may be assumed that they will crawl up to the adjacent cell and incite electric impulse over there. This may indeed be happening but if that was the exclusive way, the function of the nervous system will be very tardy. We see it operating almost in flashes and therefore, modalities other than the actual contact with a neurotransmitter substance must be occurring. For this kind of speeds, a mere chemical reaction will not suffice. It can be a quantum event involving quantum fields.

Quantum Field

A field is that region in which a force is experienced originating from one source that acts on the other bodies within a particular region. A field is space equipped with potentiality. By now we are familiar with gravitational, electrical and magnetic fields. The dimensions of the synapse as studied through electron microscope show a range wherein the quantum phenomena may occur within the limits imposed by Hiesenburg's Principle of Uncertainty. (We have seen above that the principle postulates that at the quantum level a particle may be both—a particle and a wave). In quantum field theory, particles are represented as fields.

And, Evan Walker[42], an exclusive mathematician of consciousness, states that a phenomenon called quantum mechanical tunneling should occur. Quantum mechanical tunneling is a phenomenon whereby an electron pierces through a barrier, alters the electric potential and then causes a cascade of electrons. If such quantum events were to happen, they would create

* One Angstrom is equal to 1/100,000,000 of a centimeter.

corresponding quantum electro-dynamic fields*. John Eccles[43, 44] corroborates thus:

> These spatio-temporal fields of influence are exerted by the mind on the brain in willed action... (The influence of these fields extends in the form of)...microscopic spatio-temporal activity in the neuronal net woven by the synaptic connections of ten thousand million neurons.... that are poised close to a just-threshold level of excitability.

This brings us to a point wherein the consciousness as a perceptual awareness may be different from the *quantum consciousness* at each and every cellular point in the brain and body. One definition of the consciousness is that it is an epi-phenomenon arising in the matter *de novo*. This is then the physical location of the phenomenon as well as a possible explanation as to how it occurs. One can possibly say that a unit of consciousness *is single quantum electro-dynamic field.* Even if we were to confirm in the laboratory the strong possibility of occurrence of such a field at such locations, it will still leave us with the enigma as to how an electromagnetic does or quantum electromagnetic field becomes conscious. It brings us to a further point from the definition where the consciousness arose from matter: now we say it arises from a field. All the same that would mean that the consciousness is a field that is distinctively different from what we have so far called perceptual awareness. What has been so far discussed has been in the terms of a consciousness that arises as a consequence of functioning of certain areas of brain and cannot exist without the material brain as its fundamental cause.

The idea that we have arrived at is as different as the quantum physics from classical physics. Accepting that there is a physiological basis to awareness being perceived at the cerebral level, we repeat that there is a distinctively different class of consciousness that is in the form of a field. And there are innumerable units of quantum fields at each and every cellular level as well as synapses. This leads to a multiplicity of vast number of fields generated by the quantum events all over the body. Summation of this at the individual level will give a hologram that is individual consciousness.

---

* A quantum electro-dynamic field is one that operates on account of the interactions between the elementary particles.

If the individual holographic unit of quantum consciousness were to merge with such other, it would further constitute larger and larger hologram(s) so that a single holographic pattern of collective consciousness of a group and, subsequently, that of universal consciousness, should be obvious.

Therefore, many scientists and philosophers visualize the tiniest particle of matter to be conscious. David Bohm, a theoretical physicist and a philosopher, advances his argument that is based on the nature of universe in the form of unbroken wholeness. Since our understanding of Nature is through scientific probes that explore only a certain facet of Nature, it happens to be fragmentary. The Nature reveals certain of its aspects in response to such explorations and that becomes its explicit aspect. The explicit aspect is but a fragment of the whole Nature. The other aspect of it remains hidden that is very much there as implicate order* in Nature. The explicit order in Nature is unfolded order and implicate order is enfolded and two taken together will only make it whole. Harping on his attractive and convincing thesis of implicate and explicate order in Nature, he raises a vital question concerning consciousness, thus[45]:

> Matter as a whole can be understood in terms of the notion that implicate order is the immediate and primary actuality while the explicate order can be derived as a particular, distinguished case of implicate order. Can the actual 'substance' of consciousness be understood as having the implicate order as the primary and immediate actuality? If matter and consciousness could in this way be understood together, in terms of same general notion of order, the way could be opened to comprehend their relationship on the basis of some common ground.

And after deliberating on the same in the course of the book, The Wholeness and Implicate Order, he concludes:

> Matter as a whole is to be understood ...that the substance

---

* Apart from being a theoretical physicist, David Bohm is a philosopher too. Therefore, he is greatly respected by some physicists: some view him with scorn. Certainly some of his dialogues with philosophers like Rene Weber and J. Krishnamurti do not subscribe to logical positivism. One such discussion with Krishnamurti ends as. "So this is that!"

> of 'consciousness' as implicate order is its primary and immediate actuality. The nature of cosmos, of matter.... of life and consciousness.... have been considered to be the projections of a common ground[46].

Summarizing, physics is our model of a perfect science: it has mathematical basis. But our perfect model is an incomplete* model and the part may give a glimpse of the whole; but it cannot substitute for the whole.

When Sri Aurobindo, a mystic poet, philosopher and visionary said: "The matter shall reveal the face of spirit"[47], the poetical statement was not a mere aesthetic fantasy. It was based on philosophical speculation on Darwin's theory of evolution. Taking the scientific argument of that theory further, Sri Aurobindo prophesied that the evolution shall further evolve into such explicit forms in Nature that the face of spirit—consciousness—will be obvious in the matter too. He said that about seventy years ago and David Bohm has reverberated with it some 25 years back. Should this be the case, the paradox of Einstein, Podolsky and Rosen can be explained on the basis that the *matter itself is conscious:* (taking that proposition further) *and the field of consciousness is only limited by the theory of relativity (speed of light)!* We shall discuss this in detail later to explain paranormal phenomena.†

This discussion has led us to a very important milestone. Let us recapitulate the steps that have brought us here. We began by discussing the nature of time and taken together with the anthropic principle came to understanding that its nature has to be consistent with the existence of information processing systems (units with consciousness) like us. When taken in conjunction with discussion of space, it gave us the concept of space-time continuum.

Then we have come to understand empty space as the mother field of all possibilities. It is filled with immense energy. So a small ripple or undulation in the energy-charged space does bring about the conversion of energy into materialization of matter.

---

* We say incomplete since there is still no sign of Grand Unified Theory. Physics will be perfect when this is worked out.

† If paranormal is what should generally not be observed but it still occurs, is Einstein-Podolsky-Rosen paradox also not a paranormal phenomenon?

The matter cannot manifest anything that is not contained in it. If at some stage of biological evolution the matter were to manifest consciousness as one of its properties, it must be intrinsically contained within the matter itself *ab initio*. And if the implicate order of the matter is to incorporate consciousness, one has only to find the tools by which implicate, encoded order becomes explicit and unfolded. The proof of the statement lies right in front of our eyes everywhere. That is evident in the phenomenon of life that manifests consciousness as self-emergent quality of matter.

Consciousness Redefined

Expressing itself in the form of self-conscious, personal existence, the consciousness in man is in constant interplay with the phenomenal world. Earlier we defined consciousness as awareness. Awareness may be of one's surroundings, as inferred through the sensory inputs or it may be in terms of self-reference. Putting it another way, it involves the contact between the subject and object. But now we see the advancement of the concept. The progression is that the consciousness is the emergent property of matter. And a step further, it is the fundamental attribute of all the matter; *an attribute that may be explicitly unfolded as seen in the life forms that are conscious or may be in the form of implicate order that remains unexpressed.*

When explicit and unfolded in life forms, the consciousness impinges on the Nature and moulds and modifies it. This play of consciousness in life may be a quantum electro-dynamic field (mentioned as QED hereafter), where the basic quantum currency is a single cell or a synapse. Applied to the human being, it leads to the possibility of infinite number of quantum fields. This satisfies the physical criteria that quantum mechanical theory stipulates—an infinite number of degrees of freedom to systems where quantum phenomena are taking place.

How Good is this Theory of Quantum Consciousness?

There is a widely prevalent conviction in scientists that the nature reveals only that aspect of its reality on which the inquiry is focused. A particular research suddenly brings one paradigm into focus and soon thereafter, there is more funding for research in the area, bringing a flood of fresh information and innovations in the same field. So far bio-medical research has focalized more and more on the somatic aspects of body-mind. Most of such research has been market oriented and funded by drug companies. No drug company will fund any fundamental research into health promoting programmes nor will they have anything to do with the pristine and pure nature of consciousness and how to preserve it. There are innumerable sets of empirical evidences with reference to body-mind and the realm beyond mind, but this is a particular paradigm that would impart it a special relevance. When the paradigm of the scientific inquiry will change from the mundane materialistic gains out of research to the search for the fundamental truth, then only in biomedical sciences will be a full turn towards research in the science of consciousness.

Let us review our proposition regarding consciousness from various perspectives.

Psychologists and Psychiatrists

Let us first repudiate the psychologists and psychiatrists. Psychology is based on empirical evidence that is based on a gross level. It is interpreted through a highly structured programme, which, again, is highly speculative. In that sense, psychology can be termed as a pseudo-science. The psychologists who studied the mice running around mazes or chimpanzees doing chores are totally out of context of human consciousness. Not even two human beings are alike as evident from the immune specificity. Even if the human genome contains a 15 per cent genetic overlap with the bacterium E. coli and 98.4 per cent with chimpanzee,[48] a human being is not a micro-level E. coli or to a major degree chimpanzee. Alas, a bacterium will not scream, "I am conscious". A mouse corresponds to human by 75 per cent of genes. Yet, it is commonplace abuse to call an unbecoming human being a mouse. Such data will tell us nothing about psyche in the living systems; but it may show a glimmer of all pervading consciousness.

The behaviour psychologists (John Watson, B.F. Skinner and their followers) study the behaviour patterns of the groups on the basis of motivation and productivity and so on. Even the psychologists belonging to the cognitive school depend upon the concept of perception as derived from sensorium. True to their discipline they only study psyche. They have nothing to contribute to the understanding of consciousness.

Freud and Ego Defenses

Freudian depth psychology is nothing but a speculative construct. Its validation is that it works in Western societies and plays havoc with modern civilization because of restrictive concepts of ego*, id and superego. When Freud talked about the conscious, subconscious and unconscious, he was prefixing these adjectives to mind; he had nothing to do with the self-emerging property of matter that we are discussing as consciousness. Yet, Freud's contribution to the present thesis is in his identifying various attitudes of the mind in the form that he called ego defenses (See Appendix 2). So-called defenses in fact vitiate perception. They produce clouding of mind, faulty identity of self, and blur the pristine shine of consciousness. How this helps us with the progression of our thesis will be seen later on.

Limitations of Genius of Freud

Genius of Freud contributed to the development of psychology as distinctly different discipline apart from philosophy. A genius influences several generations beyond his times. All pervasive Freudian influence is seen in the West and Freudian psychology has become a way of life so that it merits to be termed as philosophy.

Freud did have the vision of a state of *nirvana*. But his understanding of this state as a kind of negative stagnant empty state was totally false. This could not have been avoided since his concept of self was altogether constricted and devoid of any intrinsic worth. His concept of mind as an energy system working on the thermodynamic principles reflects far-reaching vision but alas! It did not make any progress. This is laid out in his famous work known as Project[49].

---

* According to Freud, ego is a psychic self that is constantly striving to strike a balance between the conflicting demands of primitive id and morally and culturally bound super-ego. Given to this ideology, self is but delicately balanced, perpetually threatened and likely to be overturned. Ego, therefore, builds self-defenses around itself, which is a fertile ground for neurosis.

How this was conceived reveals the limitations of genius of Freud who explored several mysteries of mind; but could not go beyond mind. In the moment of intense inspiration that lasted at a stretch for about three weeks, Freud wrote his *Project for a Scientific Psychology*. No sooner his inspiration waned, he got disgusted with what he had written and threw the papers into a desk drawer to write to a friend in 1898.

I have no desire at all to leave the psychology hanging in the air with no organic basis. But beyond the conviction, that there must be such a basis (cf. with Einstein's conviction that there must be grand unified theory in physics), I have nothing.

Useful as they may be in reviewing a psychiatric patient's illness, the defenses are the reflections of a mirror that has gathered dust—to use Madame Blavetsky's phrase—and are an impediment. Jarred by such distractions, the direct light of consciousness is dimmed. Or to revert back to the theory of quantum field of consciousness, its range and magnitude is diminished.

Carl Jung and Collective Consciousness

According to this concept, Carl Jung (1875-1961) postulated a collective unconscious of the herd and species. He further enunciated about a hypothetical entity as collective unconscious that pervades the human race/groups. This all-pervasive unconscious, according to Jung exercised a compelling influence over individuals through the medium of archetypal images50. Archetypal images are highly symbolic in content and they influence an individual or a clan or the entire race through the hidden meaning of their latent contents. Jung provided no empirical proofs for his attractive theory except that it works. It can be said to work on the basis that consciousness is a field of energy that is not limited by the barriers of time, space and matter.

Ken Wilber and Transpersonal School of Psychology

Today there are only a handful of eminent psychologists/ psychoanalysts, whose philosophical contributions are in resonance with our theory. Recently there is an emergence of a transpersonal school of psychology. Prominent protagonists of this school include Abraham Maslow, Gardner Murphy (1895- 1979), Gordon Allport and Ken Wilber (1947-, all contemporaries). They all belong to the present age, the *New age,* as it has come to be called in psychological circles. Abraham Maslow said about the coming of the new age:

> I consider humanistic, third force psychology to be transitional, a preparation for a still higher "Fourth Psychology", transpersonal, trans-human, centered in the cosmos, rather than in human needs and interests, going beyond humanness, identity, self-actualization and the like[51].

The school of transpersonal psychology considers consciousness as the essence of human experience. It considers the usual awake state of awareness as less than the optimal state where there is a continuous uncontrolled play of thoughts and emotions. This play distorts the perception. This in turns impairs cognition that can lead to behaviour disorders. The school accepts the possibility of an enduring state of consciousness that is free of the projections and distortions caused by the mind.

Like the quest of physicists for a general unified theory, the philosophers of transpersonal school of psychology are in search for perennial philosophy of psychology. Considering that to be the ultimate pursuit, Ken Wilber*, the youngest psychologist in this school, explores levels of consciousness lying beyond the rational egoistic mind. Exploring these levels through mystical meditative traditions, Wilber has identified more than half a dozen trans-rational (or shall we label them as *trance* rational?) states of consciousness that he terms as higher than the usual ordinary state of awareness. This is a very useful contribution to our thesis and we shall explore it further in latter chapters.

Limitations of Psychiatry

The psychiatrists need to be reminded that their "science" is not a hard-core science. Most of its foundations derive from depth psychology that is speculative. And they yield to the definition of

---

* Ken Wilber is a biochemist by formal training. He is a self-taught academician in several diverse fields, to finally emerge as a philosopher. He edits the interdisciplinary journal, *Revision.*

science as a theory that can be falsified as well and are likely to satisfy this criterion very strongly. The validation of psychiatry is in the form of large number of psychotropic drugs that seem to be modifying the perceptual quality of consciousness. But, it stops there. The only hardcore understanding of maniac-depressive psychosis—bipolar mood disorder–is that it has something to do with lithium levels in blood. If one looks at the clinical picture of depressed individual, even a child can see the dim flicker of the flame that is consciousness. And the same individual in the maniacal phase may say:

> I hadn't felt so good in years. I don't mean just physically. It was more than that. I felt bright as a button–capable of anything. It was really extraordinary. It was as though I have never been awake before.... My mind was like some wonderful precision instrument. Everything I did was right and absolutely effortless.[52]
>
> The wife of the subject as viewed this: His mind was totally blank and his ego was bloated up beyond any bounds...

And what do the psychiatrists have to tell us about the jumbled up perceptual consciousness of the schizophrenics? Is it all due to jumbled up wires? If it were only to be so, how did the "beautiful mind" of Nash come to win the Nobel Prize?

Philosophy of Materialism

The philosophers of materialist ideology are not easy to displace. However, their belief about the brain being the seat of mind as well as consciousness is proved lopsided by the advances in the material science itself. The entire body is vibrant with molecular biological events that reverberate by cybernetic pathways to constitute mind. One can set up a logical algorithmic* sequence that can lead to the derivation that the thoughts are floating biochemical molecules in the blood stream. It can further translate as thoughts being the protein molecules being synthesized as per genetic transcription. Taking the algorithm further, it shows that the perceptual

* An algorithm is a mathematical procedure by which calculations are made.

consciousness does arise in the brain but that is only a part of the phenomena. By the synaptic network the whole nervous system is capable of being conscious through a field effect: though it may not convey awareness. We shall take the argument later on.

Epistemology and Elegant Theory

All disciplines of science rest on elegant theory. In that context, philosophy is the mother of all scientific disciplines. Epistemology would define a theory into several categories ranging from superb to bad. A theory belonging to bad category would make no sense and would, therefore, be absurd to discuss. Purely speculative theories without any logical coherence and any empirical evidence, say, the Biblical cosmology and most other mythologies would belong to bad category.

Let us understand as to what is a scientific fact. A fact of science is a statement derived from elegant logic and validated from the empirical evidence of the result of an experiment conducted in a laboratory under controlled parameters. Or it is a mathematically derived theorem that later on finds its validity in experiments. Several parameters are tested against one variable and the quantitative importance of the variable is arrived at. Such a test has the characteristic of being reproducible in the same set of conditions. The experiment is repeatable elsewhere, in similar set of conditions in the hands of others.

And science is progressively advancing: in the process it frequently invalidates its previous "knowledge". The anthology of such anecdotes will merit a book. It was, indeed, elaborated in a classic[53] wherein Popper has arrived at the conclusion that falsifiability is at least a sufficient condition for a theory to be scientific. Popper would like us to believe it to be a necessary condition too. We accept that our theory as stated above is falsifiable since it is based on scientific philosophy of logical positivism and not on mathematics or experiments.

The falsifiability is put in proper perspective by David Bohm,[(54)] by advancing his theory of wholeness and implicate order. He argues that a scientific investigation testifies to the influence of a single or a group of variables given a static matrix of standard parameters. The given result is valid as far as one set of factors is studied. But the factors in Nature are innumerable. What is unfolded in a given set of experiments hides simultaneously some unrevealed part of implicate order that has not been incorporated in the experiment. He argues that the Nature in Reality is one continuous motion and science essentially studies the parts. Putting it differently, a piece of music is not the whole symphony. But a piece of music may be a pointer to the whole.

Rules of Theory Building: Epistemological Principles and Scientific Method

There are certain phenomena in Nature that cannot be explained by modern sciences. We are about to discuss them. But how shall we explain them? In such instances, statistical probabilities can lead to a theory. Or there may be a theoretical construct with some metaphysical conditions:

1. Fertile in the logical sense: It must make a difference to what you are observing and explaining;
2. Must be extensible: must have a fairly inclusive reach;
3. Must be interconnected richly with the other disciplines aside from reference to the text;
4. Must have simplicity: Invariance with respect to the transformations is the present version of simplicity in physical science;
5. Elegance must rule over the manipulation of the scientific construct;
6. The principle of causality should come into play;
7. Science is progressive, self-corrective, dynamic enterprise that subjects itself verily to the threat of falsification, to repeated changes and revision of the fundamental facts. Science no longer contains absolute truths; and
8. It should not violate the principle that there can be no causal connection between two events at different points in space if they are further apart than the distance which light can travel within the time interval between them.

Importance of Empirical Proof

Viewed so far, it makes sense to consider consciousness as a quantum field of a certain magnitude. But how shall we prove it to be true in physical world? Einstein once said that all great theories are based on simple physical occurrences. If a good theory was found workable in reality, it may still pose contradictions, like the quantum theory did with the general theory of relativity. Einstein was troubled about the apparent lack of physicality in quantum theory[55]. In a famous letter, he wrote to Max Born in 1925:

> Quantum mechanics is very impressive. But an inner voice tells me that it is yet not the real thing. The theory produces a good deal but hardly brings us closer to the secret of the old one. I am at all events convinced that He does not play dice.

Such a hunch may trigger the quest for a grand unified theory that will be all inclusive. Quantum theory does not meet with this criterion but it did not preclude the acceptance of the quantum theory, because, it worked. Where is the empirical evidence for consciousness as quantum electro-dynamic field (QED)? Keeping in mind that Einstein also said that it is good to simplify a theory; but not too far: with due humility, we consider the following as the available empirical evidence. It will, of course, have to be carried much further by future research.

4. Empirical Evidence for Consciousness as QED

1. Schrodinger's Cat Revisited

The first line of defense of the theory comes from Schrodinger's cat phenomenon and its extensions. We have seen earlier that in the above experiment, twin possibilities exist till such time that an observation is made. We also discussed as to what it means by the act of observation that collapses the wave function from twin possibilities to a single event. When it involves an observer, the consciousness of the observer is involved in the experiment. This was perplexing and the physicists elaborated the equations by involving a further set of observers.

2. Wigner's Friend Paradox

Eugene Wigner believes that observation through human

consciousness was responsible for the collapse of the wave function[56]. He elaborated the argument by incorporating one more observer in the experiment. According to him, a friend of the observer in the original experiment asks the observer whether the cat is alive or dead. Thus there is superimposition of consciousness of an additional person. Through additional set of equations, this leads us to the conclusion that a being with a consciousness must have a different role in quantum mechanics than inanimate measuring devices.

3. Everett's Friends' Paradox

Hugh Everett argued against Wigner by stating that if the consciousness of one single individual was not a sufficient cause for the collapse of the wave function in Schrodinger's cat experiment, incorporation of consciousness of n number of additional observers will also not do so. If there is a problem with a single observer, according to Everett, it persists with any number of observers.

A number of physicists, in addition to Wigner, insist that any being with consciousness can collapse the wave function. Wigner[57] emphasized the internal reference as faculty of introspection. This to him was *sine qua non* for an object to be objectively conscious. He said:

> It is in virtue of this "immanent knowledge" that he claims the right to create for himself his own objectivity.

Wolfgang Pauli was so powerful an advocate of this theory that there was a joke current in his time. Physicists were advised not to conduct any experiment when he was in their city since his very presence may influence the outcome of the experiment. Arguments by von Neumann, London and Bauer, however, also lead to introspection or self-reference as the property of consciousness. According to this interpretation, one is led to several diverse arguments as:

1. That the universe comes into existence only at the moment of individual observation. This is pure and simple solipsism that is thoroughly unscientific and absurd.
2. That the quantum event in the form of observation of

a particle like electron is the product of observation by human consciousness. There is a field of energy and interaction with the human consciousness decides whether an electron will be observed as a particle or wave. This is in consonance with consciousness being a quantum electro-dynamic field.

3. If we regard all electrons as contingent properties to some sort of multiple observations that means multiple observers may bring about multiple quantum observations. Big Bang was a quantum event. When viewed in terms of quantum possibilities, it leads to the *multiverse* theory. That means there are multiple universes. On the empirical scale, we are observing only a single universe. This leads us to the participatory anthropic principle. Simply stated, it implies that the observers with consciousness are necessary so that the universe may come to exist. This we have discussed before.
4. Reverting back to the original experiment of Schrodinger, if the interpretation of involvement of human consciousness is accepted, it is like Alice taking the first step in Wonderland. It takes us to a vast number of unforeseen possibilities. If the consciousness of a single observer were to bring into existence only a small-scale property of an electron, supposing there were to be a higher charged field of consciousness, would it not bring about quantum events of a higher magnitude?

Let us now review the alternate discipline of biological science and what that has to say. We shall once again define the dictionary before further proceedings.

4. Intelligence and Consciousness

In philosophical discussions, often there is equivocation about consciousness and intelligence. Let us say that some day; there will be a computer, which may be more intelligent than most human beings: Cray computer in 2000 was supposed to have a memory processing of 109 computations per second. An average brain has neuronal network that has intelligent processing to the power of

10^{11} assuming that one brain cell stores a single bit of information*. But technology may surpass the human range with the advances so that some computer may be more intelligent than Einstein. But no computer will ever be conscious of itself. Its intelligence may replicate sensorium, attendant motor responses, attention and 'thought'. But it can never be self-aware in the sense that a living being is nor can it have introspection.

If we were to equate intelligence and consciousness, we would soon land up in the realm of teleology, which so frequently happens in the scientific works too. Lester Smith[58] and his co-scientists, many of them Nobel laureates, equate intelligence with consciousness. In a scientific book Intelligence came first, it is argued that in the history of evolution, function has preceded the organ through which it is exercised. Assuming that intelligence is the function of the brain, why should brain be an exception? Included amongst them are the persons of the stature of Wheeler who advocates PAP and others who extend it to FAP that postulates that intelligent life shall continue to exist for ever. Its teleological implication is that the laws governing the universe exist because we are here to observe them. This is just short of inviting theologians to join the debate. Instead if we were to apply the criteria to a human being, one may say consciousness came first and conscious beings came later.

Physiology, Biochemistry and Molecular Biology Revisited

The anatomy of the brain is very precisely defined now[59,60]. We have ascribed the functions to most areas of the brain—except frontal and prefrontal cortex. The areas that are responsible for perception of consciousness are: (i) reticular activating system and (ii) cerebral cortex.

The reticular formation consists of a continuous network of nerve cells and fibers. This area of the brain is a key area in the control of several functions in the body. One part of the formation is the reticular activating system in mid-brain. The part of central reticular formation of the brainstem that extends from the

* This is for simplification. Each gene in a specific location on a chromosome has storage capacity. There are about 30,000 to 40,000 genes in a human being. The calculation of information storage thus becomes astronomical.

pons to the thalamus* profoundly influence arousal and hence, consciousness. The information is processed to the cerebral cortex through several pathways in reticular activating system. This information causes a sleeping person to be awake. The state of being awake thus depends on the intactness and activity of reticular formation. The state of awareness, if it is taken as equivalent to the state of consciousness, is dependent on the continuous projection of sensory information to the cortex. Thus intactness and integral function of cerebral cortex are necessary for awareness.

Physiologically, the states of wakefulness, sleeping and dreaming are said to be normal states of consciousness. Other states of consciousness are lethargy, stupor and coma; physiologists call them to be altered states of consciousness† v. A lethargic person (patient) is slow in speech and his voluntary movements are diminished and slow. The movements of the eyes are there but slow and the blinking is infrequent. A patient in stupor speaks only when the painful stimulus is applied. The voluntary movements are absent, the eyes are closed and there are very little spontaneous eye movements. A person in coma is unconscious. He does not speak. If painful stimulus is applied, there may be reflex mass movements of parts but there is no awareness. The eyes are closed and there is no eye movement.

Different degrees of wakefulness seem to depend on the degree of activity of reticular formation. The function of the cerebral cortex is dependent upon the inputs from the reticular activating system so that it may be said that this system lights up the cortical areas responsible for being conscious.

The case histories of patients help us to understand this clearly. Medical scientists of today are ingrained with the understanding that life is sacred and a physician must endeavor to preserve it. But the advances in material science have taken giant strides. This has changed the definition of death. Only a few decades ago, organ

---

* Broadly speaking this area may be termed as mid-brain. Mid-brain is that part of the brain that connects medulla oblongata to thalamus and cerebral cortex.

† Hypnosis and meditative states are also studied physiologically and are labeled as altered states of consciousness. The changes in the body functions during these states are extensively elaborated. But the mental and 'supra-mental' characteristics of these states are rather poorly understood.

transplantation was frowned upon. Today, it is a donation by the family of the brain dead person.

A famous controversy in public life has contributed to the general acceptance of such a fact. In 1975, Karen Quinlan[61], a young woman in USA took some drugs and cocktail. She became unconscious. She survived for ten years. She even went through the daily cycles of waking and sleep. When she died, after the ventilator support was withdrawn amidst public protests that caused a national controversy, autopsy revealed that there was a circumscribed area of dead brain confined only to her thalamus. Thalamus is situated above the area of reticular formation and its information relays to the cerebral cortex pass through it. This proved beyond any doubt that thalamus is absolutely necessary for the consciousness.

Let us see another clinical case history. A young medical student had a motorcycle accident. He was unconscious with an injury to his head. After some time, he seemed to be coming out of coma. He showed signs of being awake but he was not aware of his environment. He would open his eyes and appeared to follow people with their movements. He did not speak and did not respond to commands. He went through asleep and awake cycles but did not respond to pain. He was the same six months after. The neurological explanation was that the patient was awake but not aware. The reticular formation in the brain had survived the accident so that the patient went through asleep-awake cycles and breathed normally. But his cerebral cortex was dead and hence he would remain in vegetative state.

Both the instances taken together shows that cerebral cortex, as well as reticular formation is a physiological must for perceptual consciousness.

6. Brain Death[62] Organ Transplants

Now the criteria are very specific for the brain death. An unconscious person is brain dead after his brain is deprived of oxygen for more than three minutes. Sometimes such a person is revived between three and five minutes when his centers for consciousness die but his brain centers for the vital functions survive. The heart and the rest of the organs of the body can survive varying degree of anoxia for longer period of time. When supported by a respirator, his heart continues to beat; respiration and digestive system shall function normally for a variable period of time. Medical doctors have now prescribed clinical criteria* that are sufficient to declare a person brain dead so that live organs like heart, liver, kidneys and pancreas from such a "person", may be removed for transplantation.

Yet this dispels the previously held analogy that the brain is something like a telephone exchange. We have also discounted current fashionable analogy to it being a computer. The storage, coding, activation of coded programmes and cross-references occur at all the systemic levels. The influence pervades all the cells in the body. This causes an immense field. The nearest computer analogy would be a LAN alignment of nth number of computers (all the cells in the body, their mitochondria and genes with x number of receptors on cell membranes). Just visualize them working through innumerable synapses with their zigzag traffic in multi direction and enormous amount of software in terms of numerous messenger molecules.

Such an understanding buttresses the case for the philosophers of materialistic philosophy. Yes, this tells us one clear fact: A certain part of the brain is necessary as the seat of consciousness, and without being conscious such a person is just like a "living corpse". It also tells us that without the support of brain, life may still persist. It leaves us with a question: Is there anything like "organ consciousness" or "cellular consciousness"? Beyond that it does not contribute to our understanding of consciousness as a field. On the contrary, such arguments provide strong support for purely materialistic philosophy.

Instead let us turn to biochemistry and molecular biology for some more light. We now also know of the vast variety of

---

* They include fixed dilated or semi-dilated pupils, no response to painful stimuli, particularly to the regions around orbit, absence of corneal reflex, no eyeball movements to the syringing of the ear with 50 ml. of cold or hot water and confirmation of such findings by at least two neuro-physicians merits certification as brain dead, after three examinations at six hours interval. Of course, the person should have not been given any drugs at least 12 hours before the examination. Electroencephalogram is not mandatory. It will show a flat straight line. PET scan is not usually available but can show the exact area of the damage.

biochemical compounds in the nature of neurotropic* ubstances, hormones and such other messenger molecules. We have unraveled the mysteries of receptors on the cell membrane. Our understanding has shown mitochondria to be the powerhouses within the cell and genes as the driving engines. This gives us the picture of a cybernetic interplay of messenger molecules that turn on and turn off each other as per the needs of the body and as commanded by the genes. And we know only a little about how the arousal is brought about.

7. Early Arousal Genes and Consciousness

The arguments in favour of materialistic philosophy are further strengthened by recent developments in the understanding of arousal genes. In 1953 Watson and Crick discovered the double helix structure of the chromosomes in the cell nucleus. In 1976, Khorana decoded the structure of the gene and soon thereafter, synthesized it in the laboratory†. This has been the field of spectacular advances in biomedical sciences ever since then. By 2002 the entire human genome has been mapped out. The function of each and every gene has been assigned and the structure and location are precisely known.

This has given us the clues about the genes that bring about arousal and are, therefore, connected with consciousness.

Electrical impulses arising from thoughts, emotions and imagery arrive at the hypothalamus and undergo transduction there to produce corresponding messenger molecules[63]. For various categories of thoughts and emotions, there are different "cocktails" of molecules produced and the matrix of their influence is called a state dependent memory pattern. This matrix extends all over the body, to all the cells. And it is a two-way street. There is continuous processing of the information through cybernetic loops[64]. This established a biochemical basis to consciousness.

The influence percolates to/originates with gene expression[65]. The messenger molecules enter the cell either through the

---

* Neurotropic substances are the molecules that are secreted by the nervous system.

† A gene is composed of DNA molecules. This is the only category of protein that replicates itself. That way it is live protein.

receptors situated on the cell wall or directly migrating across the cell membrane. A category of genes, characterized as immediate early genes find their expression. First to come into action are two genes named c-fos and c-jun and they come into play within two minutes of arousal signals from the environment. They transduct these signals, by forming a transcription factor*, so as to bring appropriate gene expression of about 100 other immediate early genes. The proteins produced by the expression of these genes form a transcription factor for the activation of other genes. The action of arousal genes leads to the synthesis of dopamine from the amino acid phenyl tryptamine. Dopamine is the chemical mediator of consciousness. The genomic interplay in expression and suppression of various genes not only determines the arousal but also the behaviour. This is the genetic basis of consciousness.

The arguments in support of materialist philosophy have thus gathered tremendous ground. But this will not explain how exactly the beginning of the cybernetic connections of gene expression is brought about. Are there any quantum events involved in the switching on and off the gene expression? We do not know. The philosophers of materialism are sure that there is some switch or mechanism that turns on the "computer" and will eventually be found. And, even this will not explain who switches on the computer. Moreover, we do not know whether the quantum events are involved in the energy efficient processes of gene expression, gene transcription and gene translation.

8. *Quantum Events in Living Systems: Photosynthesis*

The parody about the science of consciousness is that most of it has been explored through molecular biology that hardly includes any study of quantum events in living systems. So much so that we may ask the question: do quantum events occur in living systems at all? If there is evidence of quantum events in human body, then we can say that it may generate a quantum electro-dynamic field.

There is one, definite evidence that they do occur in vegetable kingdom and without which, we will not be here.

---

* The genes manufacture a messenger molecule, ribonucleic acid, RNA. While this molecule carries information it is incapable of replicating itself.

This is the phenomenon of photosynthesis. During the process of photosynthesis, it may be loosely stated that light energy is transferred into chemical energy. This we know since 1771 when Joseph Priestly showed that

$$CO_2 + 2H_2O \xrightarrow{\text{light energy}} (CH_2O) + O_2 + H_2O$$

And now we know that light energy consists of photons. The photon in sunlight drives a series of electron transfers that occurs through the energy currency of living systems, viz. adenosine triphosphate compound. The ration of energy stored is directly proportional to the quanta of light absorbed. The equation that produces carbohydrates from carbon dioxide is driven by chlorophyll but it is entirely light dependent as:

$$6CO_2 + 12H_2O \xrightarrow{\text{Photon}} C_6H_{12}O_6 + 6O_2 + 6H_2O$$

The photon does get "absorbed" into molecules concerned but cannot be shown in the equations as actively participating since it is a subatomic entity while the chemical reactions occur at molecular level. That the carbohydrates are necessary for survival of entire living systems is commonplace understanding.

That quantum events do occur in the vegetable kingdom is of paramount importance. And there is indirect evidence of there being some kind of field about the plant kingdom. A leaf from which a part is torn shows as whole leaf through Kirilean photography. This kind of photography photographs the objects as well as fields.

What may be deduced is that quantum events may be occurring in the higher forms of living systems too. And in so doing, they might be generating field effects. This may be consciousness itself. Is there a field around human existence? Let us see.

8. Electromagnetic Field between Two Hands

Rossi uses a common phenomenon that is easily demonstrable for induction of hypnosis. That is the development of a field between two hands (Fig. 3.4). Anybody can experience it as follows:

> Hold the two hands about 14 inches apart and keep gazing at them steadily while you move them slowly to and fro for

> a few inches at a time. As you do this, you find that there is some force of attraction between your two hands and it is becoming a bit more difficult to draw them a part. After a few minutes, they are drawn nearer and nearer to each other and eventually they may clasp. At that point it may require some force to separate them.

A physicist's explanation is that two hands work as two end plates of a charged body connected in circuit and exhibit positive and negative charge. This draws them together. And with sophisticated gadgets, it should be possible to quantify the field between two hands. The potential of the field is likely to be small, but with sensitive device, it should be measurable. We are searching for it.

The explanation provides a simple proof of the body being a charged object generating electro-dynamic field. Similar other proofs are in the electrocardiogram and electroencephalogram. Since there are electric potentials in the body, of course, they will generate electromagnetic field. However, this may or may not correlate with quantum electro-dynamic (QED)* field.

This led to an interesting interaction with Ernest Rossi. The phenomenon is displayed poignantly on the cover of the book, The Symptom Path to Enlightenment[66] with the editor of the book, Kathryn demonstrating the Phenomenon. We wrote to Rossi asking permission to reproduce the image.

Rossi replied:

Your book on the quantum electro-dynamic field sounds interesting. I wonder if you have referenced my work in this area as it appeared in my book "Dream, Consciousness, and Spirit: The Quantum Experience of Self-Reflection and Co-Creation." (2002, Zeig, Tucker, & Theisen, Phoenix: Arizona).

---

* When the electromagnetic radiation interacts with charged subatomic particles, a quantum electromagnetic (QED) field is said to be generated.

We answered as follows:

We may point out the kind of answers our hypothesis will generate to the observations that you have sent. They are:

Rossi 1: "If a person tries to observe what he is thinking about at the very moment that he is reflecting on a particular subject, it is generally agreed that he introduces unpredictable and uncontrollable changes in the way his thoughts proceed thereafter. Why this happens is not definitely known."

Our answer is that there is superimposition of different quantum fields and the non-coherence between them produces interference between several QEDs that generate as per the various thought processes in different locations.

This kind of interference is a common experience and therefore, Patanjali in his treatise advises the practice of a kind of "mental exercise". All varieties of meditative programmes require *pratyahar* or *pratikraman*. That literally means focal attention and fading away of the marginal area.

Rossi 2: "After all, what could an interference pattern in light or water (or any other medium) possibly have in common, with cognitive patterns of self-reflection, such as thought, attitudes, emotions, sensation, perception, and behaviour? If this were true, that would explain the pathological cognitive dysfunction in the brain of a schizophrenic. Can they interfere with each other just as physical quanta-such as subatomic particles and photons (light quanta) do in the classical double-slit experiment?"

Our Response:

Yes, QED will explain this as the interference between two asynchronous fields. By the same token, there can be a potentiation between the fields by their congruence. This explains creativity and various numinous kinds of experiences that you and Jung have described-and for that matter all meditators have experienced (Fig. 3.4).

Rossi 3: "You need two events. Consciousness is the relationship between two events *via* this quantum-physical mechanism... I suggest that the conscious field is the product of these two quantum waves and this product appears as a probability field that exists everywhere, not just in the brain, but everywhere."

Fig. 3.4: Electromagnetic Field between Two Hands

Source: Demonstration of a field between two hands through kind courtesy of Ernest and Kathryn Rossi.

Our Response:

QED operates at all synapses in the body so not only there may be two events; there is infinite degree of freedom, which is a prerequisite in quantum physics, for n number of quantum fields to interact. Of course, yes, at all places where quantum events may be happening in the body—all synapses and energy exchange processes like adenosine triphosphate being converted to diphosphate will, in the process, give up one energy bond. The entire body is, therefore, numinous and a QED field.

Rossi 4: "...Other analogies between the quantum dynamics of all the elementary particles of the universe and human thought consist of the relations between the part and the whole, logic and causality, stages of the creative process, and "the quantum jump"—that is, the shift from the potential to the actual that we experience when a sensation, perception, emotion, or idea suddenly emerges into consciousness. The experience of conscious choice corresponds to a quantum jump or what is also called the collapse of the wave function, wherein the infinite potentials of quantum reality are suddenly actualized into a single experience."

Our Response:

This collapse of the wave function is the synergetic superimposition of corresponding fields—QED fields that have been produced by the chaotic functioning of the brain before the actual event of collapse of the wave function. This is the generic ground for creativity and insight, in fact, of all important discoveries and inventions.

We provide further answers from the meditative way of Patanjali as well as from the *Vajrayana* Buddhist meditation.

We must all the same keep in mind that these are qualitative statements. At best it is a hypothesis that is further limited by not having any quantifiable mathematical or physical basis, as yet.

We have thus explored the veracity of the emerging paradigm of consciousness being a QED. There are several indicators in physics that it may be so. However the biological sciences support a strong materialist position based on molecular biological events. The synthesis is that should QED be established as the physical nature of consciousness, it will further support the materialist position. That would, however, explain some of the phenomena in consciousness that do occur and are unexplained so far. We shall review such data later.

The Data Unexplainable so far: Physicists are hard to please! The logic can jump by algorithmic sequence. While the philosophers would delight at such insights as quantum jump, the physicists will insist on quantification and experimental proofs. What Einstein has said mathematically, over 90 years ago, is still subjected to experimental validation.

For this reason, we have tried to make all statements as accurate as possible and within the range of the dictionary meaning attached to the words of a particular discipline. We sorely miss the quantification through mathematics and laboratory data. But we are believers in the philosophical speculations and think that such speculations may indeed be insights. Idea is one of the several things that cannot be analyzed. We resort to Heisenberg's retort to his critics when he said: "I do not need to answer such questions because you cannot ask such a question experimentally." Dirac is said to have "answered" in a similar vein when someone from the audience asked a long-winded question and Dirac stood silently. When the Chairman pointed out to Dirac that they were waiting for him to answer, Dirac said that he was waiting for the question to be framed in the same terms as the answer was sought.

We find the reconciliation in the simple statement by Feynman that the basis of science is its ability to predict and to predict means to tell what will happen in an experiment that has never been done[67].

If thoughts and memories are also electromagnetic fields, what is the mechanism of storage of such fields? So far the mechanism of storage of short and long term memories has been well documented. It occurs through new protein synthesis in the brain. The twin combination will mean that during protein synthesis for the storage of memories in the brain, a QED is brought about.

Support for such a hypothesis comes from the area of artificial intelligence. A microbe that thrives in one of the most inhospitable environments on earth might just help engineers build the first quantum computers. The highly organized building skills of a protein, manufactured by the microbe that lives in scalding sulphurus geothermal springs, has allowed NASA scientists to create regular arrays of "quantum dots". Physicists believe that quantum states of electrons can be used as quantum bits-qubits—for encoding data in a super fast quantum computer. A group of them could be harnessed to carry out many calculations simultaneously. If this were to be achieved, there shall emerge continuity from the non-living proteins to consciousness *via* qubits. DNA has already provided us with a kind of protein that is responsible for life. Proteins, as qubits that can cause QEDs to occur, will provide the link to the epiphenomenona of emergence of consciousness in matter and that way, may be, a computer may become self-conscious. *The only difference between the artificial intelligence of a robot and the human intelligence would then be that a robot would require to be switched on.*

Let us summarize our dialectical discussion about consciousness and see the emergence of a new paradigm from the creative field between the discursive streams. Our discussion at the materialistic philosophical plane is based on data obtained from the disciplines of physiology and clinical medicine based thereon, biochemistry, molecular biology of genes, psychology and quantum physics. It brings us to a strong materialist position that the brain is the principal material cause of consciousness. However, there is no clear understanding from the material sciences as to how consciousness is brought about.

While the Freudian and Jungian schools of psychology barely transcend the duality of body and mind, they have very little to contribute to the understanding of the nature of consciousness. The notable exception is the concept of archetypes and collective consciousness; however, there is no scientific explanation about them from these schools. The Fourth school of psychology propounds transpersonal and cosmic links which is an attractive hypothesis. But that also requires validation. Molecular biological events help to eliminate the body-mind dualism. They tend to make us believe that consciousness is just a substratum to the play of molecular biology: thus buttressing the materialist position.

A voice of subtle dissent emerges from the biochemical event of photosynthesis: it indicates the possibility of quantum events in higher forms of life. A review of what happens at the synapses in the transmission of an electrical impulse opens up the likelihood of generation of a quantum electro-dynamic field over there and as a corollary, all over the body. It will still be a materialist proposition but so much the better since it will be based on empirical evidence.

Arrival here we call, as the first step, by Alice in Wonderland. A quantum event has different parameters for space and time. On that basis we take the hypothesis further. *Consciousness is a QED field that forms a continuum as space-time-consciousness.* Biologically that seems plausible. Viewed as an additional dimension, it will require further substantiation in the form of empirical data and elegant mathematical proofs to call it The Fifth Dimension.

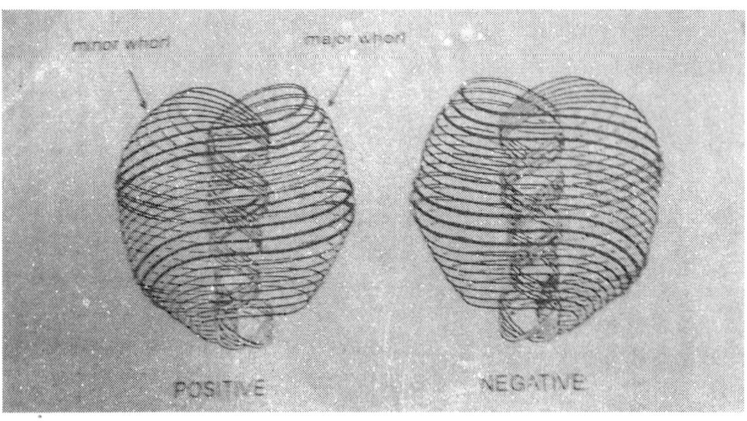

Fig. 3.5: Micro-psi Perception of Annu

Such a proposition will explain most of the paranormal phenomena. It will still have to explain as to what is involved in maintenance, storage and transmission of the quantum electro-dynamic field. And, the facts as we have seen so far, scientific as they are, still have to answer so many queries about various phenomena that are within the realm of consciousness. That we shall now discuss in the next chapter.

Fig. 3.6: Vajrasattva Buddha

ENDNOTES

1. Stephan Hawking (1989). *A Brief History of Time: From the Big Bang to Black Holes*, New York.
2. Penrose Roger (1989). *The Emperor's New Mind: Concerning Computers, Minds and the Laws of Physics*. New York.
3. Feynman, R.P. (1996). *Feynman Lectures on Physics*, New Delhi. pp. 1422-23.
4. Gleik James (1989). *Chaos, Making of a New Science*, Harmondsworth.
5. Stewart Ian (1989). *Does God Play Dice? The Mathematics of Chaos*, Oxford.
6. Penrose Roger (1989). *The Emperor's New Mind: Concerning Computers, Minds and the Laws of Physics*. New York, p. 198.
7. *Ibid.*, pp. 375-378.
8. Laurikainen, K.V. (1996). *The Message of the Atoms*, Berlin: Springer, pp. viii, 2, 41-47.

9. Lorentz, A.; Einstein, A.; Minkowski, H. and Weyle, H. (1952). *The Principles of Relativity*, New York, p. 75.
10. Gary Zukav (1979). *The Dancing Wu Li Masters: An Overview of the New Physics*, New York and London, p. 176.
11. Stephan Hawking (1989). *A Brief History of Time: From the Big Bang to Black Holes*, New York.
12. Stephan Hawking (1993). In: *Predicting the Future* ed. Leo Howe and Alan Wain, Cambridge, p. 17.
13. Alan Isaacs, *A Dictionary of Physics*, Oxford, p. 334.
14. Stephan Hawking (1989). *A Brief History of Time: From the Big Bang to Black Holes*, New York, pp. 121, 183, 194.
15. *Ibid.*, p. 194.
16. Jayant Narlikar (2003). "Science and speculation: Behind the veil of cosmology", *The Times of India*, 2 May, 2003.
17. Kroger, W.S. (1963). *Clinical and Experimental Hypnosis*, Philadelphia, pp. 15-17.
18. Rossi, E.L. (1996). *The Symptom Path to Enlightenment: The New Dynamics of Self-Organization in Hypnotherapy*, Pacific Palisades.
19. Richard I. Thomson (1977). *Consciousness and the Laws of the Nature*, Boston.
20. Fritjof Capra (1976). *The Tao of Physics: An Exploration of the Parallels between Modern Physics and Eastern Mysticism*, London.
21. Gary Zukav (1979), *The Dancing Wu Li Masters: An Overview of the New Physics*, Bungay, Suffolk.
22. Larry Dossey (1982). *Space, Time and Medicine*, Boulder and London, 1982.
23. *Ibid.*, pp. 45.
24. Barrow, J.D. and Tippler, F.J. (1996). *The Anthropic Cosmological Principle*, Oxford, pp. 17-23.
25. M. Jammer (1974). *The Philosophy of Quantum Mechanics*, New York.
26. Schulman, L.S. (1981). *Techniques and Application for Path Integration*, New York.
27. Barrow, J.D. and Tippler, F.J. (1996). *The Anthropic Cosmological Principle*, Oxford, pp. 472-494.
28. Stephen Hawking and Roger Penrose (1994). *The Nature of Space and Time*, New York, p. 134.
29. Barrow, J.D. and Tippler, F.J. (1996). *The Anthropic Cosmological Principle*, Oxford, pp. 17-23.
30. *Ibid.*, pp. 472-494.

31. E.O. Wilson (1998). *Consilience: The Unity of Knowledge*, New York.
32. Renee Weber (1973). *Dialogues with Scientists and Sages: The Search for Unity*, New York, pp. 234-41.
33. Roger Penrose (1990). *The Emperor's New Mind*, London, pp. 325-329.
34. A. Einstein, B. Podolsky and Nathan Rosen (1935). "Can quantum mechanical reality be considered complete?" *Physical Review* 47, pp. 777.
35. P.A Schilpp (1949). ed. Louis de Broglie In: *Albert Einstein: Philosopher-Scientist*, La Salle, p. 113.
36. Gary Zukav (1979). *The Dancing Wu Li Masters: An Overview of the New Physics*, Bungay, Suffolk, p. 176.
37. Goleman Daniel (1997). *Healing Emotions, Conversations with the Dalai Lama on Mindfulness, Emotions and Health*, Boston, pp. 107-144.
38. Pert, Candace, Ruff, M.R., Weber, R.J. and Herkenham, M. (1985). "Neuropeptides and their receptors: A psychosomatic network", *The Journal of Immunology*, pp. 820-826.
39. The Dalai Lama (1999). *Consciousness at Crossroads*; Conversations with the Dalai Lama on Brain Science and Buddhism Ed. Zara Houshmand, New York, pp. 16-31.
40. Patricia Churchland (1984). *Matter and Consciousness*, Cambridge, Mass.
41. James Watson (1970). *Molecular Biology of the Gene*, Menlo Park, California, pp. 67-105.
42. Walker, Evan (1970). "The nature of consciousness", *Mathematical Biosciences*, 7:131-78.
43. John Eccles (1970). *Facing Reality*, New York.
44. *Ibid.* (1973). *The Understanding of the Brain*, New York.
45. David Bohm (1984). *The Wholeness and Implicate Order*, London, pp. 48-62; 196-213.
46. *Ibid.*, pp. 193-210.
47. Sri Aurobindo (1990). *Savitri: A Legend and a Symbol*, Pondicherry.
48. Steve Jones, Robert Martin, David Pilbeam and Sarah Bunney (eds.) (1992). *The Cambridge Encyclopedia of Human Evolution*, Cambridge, p. 310.
49. Freud, S. (1966). *Standard Edition of Complete Psychological Works of Sigmund Freud*, London.

50. Jung, C.G. (1964). "Approaching the unconscious", In: *Man and His Symbols*, Garden City, p. 18.
51. Maslow, A.H. (1971). *Farther Reaches of Human Nature*, New York.
52. Goodman, L.S. and Gilman, A (1975). *The Pharmacological Basis of Therapeutics*, New York, p. 196.
53. Popper, Karl (1968). *The Logic of Scientific Discovery*, London.
54. Bohm, David (1984). *Wholeness and Implicate Order*, London, pp. 140-71.
55. Roger Penrose (1990). "The Paradox of Einstein, Podolsky and Rosen", In: *The Emperor's New Mind*, London, pp. 361-378.
56. Weigner, E.P. (1962). *The Scientist Speculates: An Anthology of Partly Baked Ideas*, New York, p. 294.
57. Weigner, E.P. (1963). *Am. J. Phys*. 31, 6.
58. Lester Smith, (ed.) (1975). *Intelligence Came First*, London.
59. Snell, R.S., *Clinical Neuroanatomy: The Structure and Functional Localization of the Cerebral Cortex*, pp. 289-297, 302, 352, 441, 502-3.
60. Totora, G.J. (1999). *Principles of Anatomy and Physiology, Integrative Functions of Cerebrum*, pp. 517-19.
61. Fackelmann, K.A. (1994). "The conscious mind", *Science News*, 146; 10-11.
62. John Walton (2000). *Brain's Diseases of Nervous System: The Diagnosis of Brain Death*, pp. 134-142.
63. Pert Candace (1998). *Molecules of Emotions*, London, pp. 19-71, 131-148.
64. Pert Candace *et al*. (1989). "Self reflective molecular psychology", *Psychological Perspectives*, 20, 213-221.
65. Rossi, E.L. (2002). *The Psychobiology of Gene Expression*, New York, pp. 235-38.
66. Rossi, E.L. and Rossi K.L. (1996). *The Symptom Path to Enlightenment*, Pacific Palisades.
65. Feynman, R.P. (1996). *Feynman Lectures on Physics*, New Delhi, p. 1422.

4
Tibetan Buddhist Perspective

So far we have explored space, time and consciousness through Scientific Mode. We have seen that this mode has led us to a physical concept of space-time-consciousness being an additional dimension. There is no question of a final answer about the ultimate reality since empirical validation is yet to come. Moreover, scientific mode, *per se*, accepts a future modification through further research. We have also reflected upon the apparent paradoxes within the compass of the scientific mode as well as some of the phenomena that are unexplained. We have found reconciliation by advancing a hypothesis. Now let us examine Tibetan Buddhist Tradition since it has certain postulates that seem to correlate with our hypothesis.

The Buddhist tradition is firmly rooted in the fundamental teachings of Siddharth Gautama, who on attaining enlightenment became Buddha. We shall only dwell on the postulates of Tibetan Buddhism. It provides a well-charted course to access the fifth dimension. That gateway to the fifth dimension is through the meditative way. This is common to all Buddhist practices and Zen Buddhism though the techniques differ.

Tibetan Buddhism belongs to the Mahayana school. This school lays great emphasis on the virtue of compassion for all sentient beings. On the path to Enlightenment, even those Exalted Ones—*Bodhisattvas*—who could possibly pass on to the higher realms of Buddhahood, would not do so out of compassion for their fellow beings. They would prefer to revert back to the *samsara*, the material world so that they may help. The Classic prayer for the practitioners of Mahayana Buddhism, as the Dalai Lama says, is as follows:

> For as long as space endures,
> And for as long as living beings remain,

Until then may I too abide
To dispel the misery of the world.[1]

Vajrayana in Tibetan Buddhism provides blueprints of the pathways in the meditative practices. In the course of meditation, a fourth state of awareness, that is quite different from the commonly experienced three states, awareness, sleep, and dreaming, is induced. And it is through this kind of gateway that we are going to have the glimpse of space-time-consciousness continuum. We shall discuss meditative practices in some detail. But we should study the philosophical postulates first.

Buddhist Cosmology

The cosmological view here is that time is timeless, without a beginning and without an end. Space is limitless and it is an energy field. The consciousness, like time, has continuity and is eternal. It is indestructible and undergoes transmutation from one sentient being to other in a chain of cyclical existence that stops only at *nirvana*[2]. The validation of these concepts is through a system that is almost akin to logical positivism/empiricism.

This logical system is known as *four principles* of examining any phenomenon for its veracity. They are:

1. *Principle of reality:* Certain phenomena exist by virtue of their luminosity and convey intrinsic truth, e.g. consciousness exists. That just *is*.
2. *Principle of dependence:* Here it is necessary to understand the relation of the phenomena to grasp the real nature.
3. *Principle of efficacy.* This means to ascertain that a certain cause brings about a certain effect and see the functioning of the causes as operant in the effects and their sequence.
4. *Principle of valid proof.* This is inclusive of the above three and the progression of logical sequence there from that examines relationship between propositions and empirical data and generates hypothesis.

Let us explore the Buddhist metaphysics along these lines and look for validation/contradictions.

The Buddha's teachings were simple as well as profound. They can be easily summarized in the form of (i) Four Noble Truths, (ii) Twelve-fold Chain of Causation of Suffering, (iii) Eightfold Path of Righteous Living, (iv) The doctrine of emptiness and non-ego (*anatmana*) and (v) *nirvana*[3]. First three are simple enough to understand and are useful as a prelude to the meditative way. Our present endeavor is to examine the last two concepts in cosmological terms.

The Doctrine of Non-Ego (Anatmana)

Buddha at the time of his death is said to have predicted the birth of a *Bodhisattva* four hundred years thereafter. Nagarjuna[4] is said to be the same monk. Nagarjuna is the first and foremost in the Mahayana tradition to expound it to its philosophical heights.

The philosophy follows both ways, i.e. that of logical positivism as well as nihilism. Nagarjuna postulates that (i) the cosmos is without a beginning and without an end. It arose from *sunyata.* Thus, *Sunyata*—emptiness is the mother field of all possibilities. All the phenomena arise from *sunyata* and are related as cause and effect. Therefore, the phenomenal world is interdependent and interconnected. So, all phenomena follow the doctrine of *pratityasamutpada,* i.e. for their existence they are dependent on some preceding cause. Though all the phenomena do exist in conventional reality they are devoid of any independent intrinsic content.

(ii) Through the path of denouncing all phenomena as intrinsically devoid of any independent existence, one can negate the entire chain of cosmological events on the basis of the principle of causality and change: unless one invokes a primordial cause. If emptiness is all-empty, there is no primordial cause. In this nihilistic way too, Nagarjuna leads us to the doctrine of *sunyata,* i.e. emptiness. Emptiness is all-void; it is empty of itself too[5].

The thrust of the philosophy is that in the phenomenal world, there is intimate link between the cause and effect (*karmic* connection). Causality and change are connected, as we think about hem in Newtonian physics. Nothing exists by itself alone. It exists n correspondence and is interconnected[6].

Emptiness of Emptiness[7]

I there is no independent existence of any phenomenon, there can be no reality to any phenomenon, physical or mental. So the Buddhist tradition refutes the existence of any real physical or mental images of the world: yet, as they seem to exist, they do so as dependently related events on the aggregate/associated phenomena. There is a paradox here.

A scholar named Bhavaviveka pointed this out[8]. He pointed out that if any of the phenomena conventionally exists in its own right that cannot be said to be empty of true existence. If it were to be assumed, that the phenomena exist in their own right that leads to denial of the principle of dependent origination, principle of cause and effect - this will be paradoxical. This will be a violation of the axiomatic clause and that cannot be. This is because of the basic postulate, that an effect in order to come into existence must of necessity have a cause.

The contradiction is resolved by explaining that what we see as existence in physical and mental world does appear so, because of its own attributes that go along with its existence, *just as the reflection in a mirror is dependent on the attributes of there being a reflecting surface as well as an object being reflected.* For elucidating the point more clearly, let us now take resort to a dialogue by Bhadrapala, a monk of the Madhyamaka* School with Buddha. The story goes on as:

Buddha: Bhadrapala, when you wish to see fine features of your face, what do you do?

Bhadrapala: I take up a vessel full of refined oil, or clean water, or I look into a crystal or to a mirror.

Bhadrapala, do you think what you see in any of these four objects has already been in existence there?

No.

So is it to be regarded altogether as non-entity?

No.

Is it to be regarded as being within any of them?

No!

---

* This is the school that advocates avoidance of extremes and advises the choice of the middle way. The Buddha after undertaking fast for several days did not get enlightenment. He got it when a shepherd girl gave him a glass of milk. Thereafter he taught *madhyamapratipada, the* path of the middle way. The profound philosophy of the middle way was propounded by Nagarjuna, about five hundred years after Buddha's *nirvana.*

Is it to be regarded as outside of them?

No.

Then what is the image? Where does it come from?

To this Bhadrapala replied: As the oil, water, crystal and mirror are clear, transparent and free from muddiness and dust, the image is reflected in them. Neither the image comes out of the object, nor does it get into them from outside; nor is it there by itself, nor is it artificially constructed. The image comes from nowhere, vanishes away to nowhere; it is not subject to birth and death; it has no fixed abode.

To this Buddha said: so it is, as you said, Bhadrapala. When objects are pure and clean, the image is clearly reflected in them. So it is with Bodhisattva. When he meditates on Buddhas* with singleness of thought, he sees them; having appeared to him they stay with him; staying with him they explain things to him he wishes to understand. Being thus enlightened by them, he is delighted; he now reflects: whence do these Buddhas come from? And whither does this body of mind vanish? When he thus reflects, he sees that all the Tathagatas come from nowhere and go out to nowhere. So it is with my own body, he realizes, it has no definite path by which it comes, and how can there be any returning to anywhere?

The story illustrates the point that there is no intrinsic reality to the physical self though we do experience various qualities within this reflection. There is another argument in support of non-self. The obvious physical self, though an instrument of our functionality, cannot be our real self since it changes every moment. A person at the particular age or moment has been different in the past because his physical and mental aggregates have been constantly changing. This seemingly solid, concrete, independent, self-instituting, I, under its own power that appears at any one time, actually does not exist at all, and this specific non-existence is what is meant by selflessness[9]. There is no *self*: instead, the real nature of self is non-self (*anatmana*)†.

---

* It is a common mistake to think of only one Buddha. Siddharth Gautama became a Buddha on attaining enlightenment. But there can be countless number of Buddhas and all of us have the potentiality to become one.

† This concept is in sharp contradiction to the Freudian concept of ego as well as the Indian Classical concept of *atman*. *Atman* is equivalent

At this juncture, it is appropriate to define our vocabulary. In Buddhism, mind is not equivalent to psyche, ego is not equivalent to self and the Freudian concepts of conscious mind, subconscious mind and unconscious mind are also alien. But according to the tradition mind is classified into two categories, coarse mind and subtle mind. Coarse mind is the dialectical faculty of intellect. It reflects like a mirror only and if there is dust on the mirror, the reflection is distorted to that extent. The subtle mind carries the refined imprints of the being and is the consciousness that departs at death. It can then exist somewhere in the realm called *bardo*. After persisting there for some indefinite time, it is reborn as another individual. Some of the qualities of subtle mind therefore are of necessity present in the reincarnation.

This brings us to another paradox. The Buddhist tradition firmly believes in reincarnation. If there is no real physical or mental self, what is it that reincarnates? If there is no intrinsic existence of any phenomena, how does subtle mind exist of its own? How does it persist in *bardo** and how does it take rebirth? We do not have the answers as per logical positivism. Even if the subtle mind were to be a quantum electro-dynamic field, it cannot explain all the phenomena associated with the theory of rebirth. In terms of empiricism, if the data of Stevenson and like, as well as the very institution of the Dalai Lama, were to provide empirical proofs, we still will have to discover so much more in natural laws to understand that.

We still have to answer to the materialist philosophy. We have to explain the contribution of physical factors like the brain and nervous system in the causation of mental events and in the functioning of the subtle mind. Mental events, Buddhism accepts, could not have taken place without the co-operating contribution of the brain etc. But brain is not the substantial cause of the consciousness. Axiomatically, consciousness is without a beginning and without an end. If it arose from *the void* it can vanish only

to the concept of soul. It is a part of the Ultimate Reality, *paramatman*. That way it differs in Tibetan concept. But its similarity to the Tibetan concept is that it is *atman* that reincarnates. This way *atman* is similar to the subtle mind of the Tibetan tradition.

* A hypothetical astral field between the world and areas that lead to *nirvana*.

when it returns to that void. In any sentient being, it just finds its expression by the brain. How does the consciousness return to the eternal void? *Nirvana* explains that to us.

Nirvana

Considering that subtle mind is the consciousness and that undergoes a cyclical chain of birth-death and rebirth, refinement of the subtle mind through righteous living brings that consciousness to a level when it can avoid rebirth. This is the state of *nirvana.*

Following the meditative way, one arrives at a profound experience. The experience has been variously described as communion in consciousness, a timeless moment, the Nameless Experience[10] etc. It is the experience of *sunyata.* The experience is the realization of a state that is devoid of any contents. Such an experience can be had momentarily at the culmination of meditation for a while but staying constantly in this realm of selflessness leads to complete freedom from all gross and subtle imprints. There is a true experience of the nature of reality. Complete dissolution of gross and subtle aggregates of the mind leads to a state of enlightenment.

The dissolution of even the subtle mind that we may call a special kind of consciousness into "some unknown unfathomable realm" from which there is no return, is *nirvana.* Poetically expressed:

> Misery only doth exist, none miserable,
> Nor doer is there; naught save the deed is found,
> *Nirvana* is, but not the man who seeks,
> The path exists, but not the traveler on it. 140

Space, Time and Consciousness in Buddhism

The Buddhism has a cyclic view of time.[11] In Buddhist traditions there are infinite world systems, each with its own Buddhas and Buddhism. Buddhist cosmology presents a relatively stable and predictable world, a closed but potentially infinite future. All natural phenomena are devoid of any intrinsic content. Therefore, there is no time, but there is only all-abiding timelessness, there is no space but there is all-pervasive void, which is full of energy.

In the limitless expanse of timelessness, there exists void space, surcharged with energy. A little undulation in the energy field brings forth the birth of Universe.

The consciousness too originates from the void. In the sphere of emptiness (*nirvana*), the consciousness ceases to be. But that shall happen not at the time of brain death. When the consciousness reverts back, to the eternal void that is the stage of *nirvana*.

Thus the concepts of space and time are almost identical between the Buddhist cosmological view and modern scientific mode of thinking. When it comes to consciousness, there is a sharp contradiction. Logical positivism/empiricism cannot bridge that gap[12].

But then, if the paranormal phenomena as we have discussed, are a reality, they cannot be explained by logical positivism either. This makes the limitations of the theory of logical positivism obvious. Of course, science is much more than logical positivism. While most of the laws of nature can be explained on the basis of logical positivism, there are innumerable paradoxes/facts in all scientific disciplines that are not explained by logical positivism. In quantum physics we have seen logical inconsistency. Moreover there are other phenomena that are unexplained. So, even the principle of confirmation of the theory by empirical data does not work.

It is not implied that logical inconsistency should be ignored. But it is argued that irrefutable evidence is not discarded because it lacks explanation. In the scientific pursuit the remedy is by further accumulation of data and advancement/falsification of the theory. When such data that does not confirm to the theory presents itself, we need a paradigm shift.

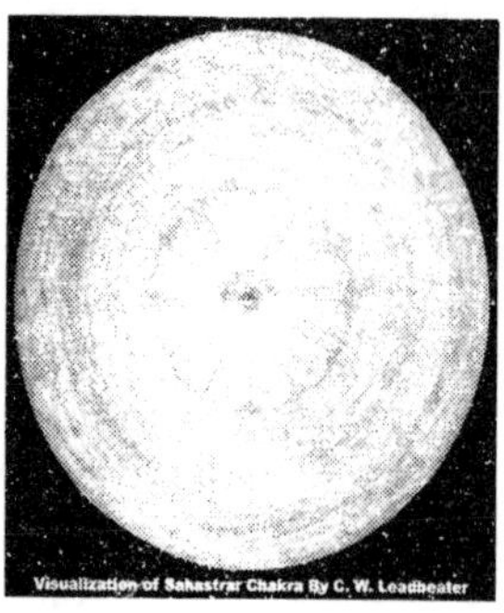

Fig. 4.1: Sahasrar Chakra

The present status of research about consciousness is mostly through material sciences. And that is unlikely to explain the paranormal phenomena that do not easily lend themselves to research investigations. Let us explore the alternative path of meditative way. Subjective as it is, it parallels with intuition and generation of insight.

ENDNOTES

1. The Dalai Lama (1990). *Freedom in Exile*, London, p. 297.
2. Dalai Lama (1995). *The World of Tibetan Buddhism*, Boston, pp. 29-30, 48, 51-53, 100.
3. Suzuki, D.T. (1980). *Essays in Zen Buddhism*, First Series, London, p. 48.
4. Kensur Lekden (1998). *Nagarjuna in Meditations of a Tibetan Tantrik Abbot*, Dharmashala, pp. 74-80.
5. Huntington, C.W. Jr. and Geshe Namgyal Wangichen (1989). *The Emptiness of Emptiness*, Honolulu, p. 190.
6. The Dalai Lama (1995). *The World of Tibetan Buddhism*, Boston, p. 34.
7. The Dalai Lama (1991). *Path to Bliss: A Practical Guide in the Stages of Meditation*, Ithaca, pp. 42-45, 87, 101, 143-48, 172.
8. Kensur Lekden (1998). *Nagarjuna in Meditations of a Tibetan Tantrik Abbot*, Dharmashala, pp. 74-80.
9. Kensur Lekden (1985). *Kindness, Clarity and Insight*, Ithaca, New York, p. 70.
10. Rohit Mehta (1978). *J. Krishnamurty and The Nameless Experience*, Delhi.
11. Richard Gombrich (1993). *Buddhist Prediction: How open is the Future, in Predicting the Future*, ed. Leo Howe and Allan Wain, New York, p. 149.
12. Hayward, J.W. and Varela, F.J., (1992). *Gentle Bridges, Conversations with the Dalai lama on the Sciences of Mind*, Boston, pp. 17-24.

5
Meditative Way: Raj-Yoga of Patanjali

How do we validate the metaphysical data? It is obvious that logical positivism cannot provide us with the answers here.

There is a subjective experience that parallels with intuitive realization. Intuitionism as a school of thought is appreciated in Eastern and Western Philosophy—Gestalt psychology and the moment of enlightenment in existentialist philosophy of Kierkegaard[1]. The Tibetan as well as Classical Indian concepts derive their validation not only along the logical steps to a certain extent, but also through intuitive experience. As we have seen, there is no convergence between the materialistic philosophical concepts of what is self and consciousness. Apparently the scientific concepts have dominated the global civilization in twentieth century. The world revolves around the concept of self. The values are autonomously derived from this concept and they operate at various levels of mind. The institutions are built on the foundations of values and they constitute the pillars of the civilization. That not just guides the life styles and matrix of culture, but is also the generic ground of conflicts. Such conflicts are at all levels, from the individual's own environment to global situations. Therefore, the modality of the conflict resolution must of necessity revert back to the values derived from the concept of self. Then they have to be cherished, nurtured, preserved and protected[2].

The pathway for the appreciation of the concepts of Mahayana Buddhism, Vajrayana and Indian Classical tradition[3, 4, 5*] is well

---

* For the exposition of the Indian Classical Tradition that follows, the main stay is Patanjali's Yoga Sutra. We have relied heavily on three commentaries on this masterpiece. 1. Yoga: *The Art of Integration* by Rohit Mehta, 2. *The Science of Yoga* by I.K. Taimni. 3. *Indian Philosophy* by S. Radhakrishnan, Vol. two.

charted. But its mainstay is the experience. It begins by transforming our ordinary consciousness to an altered state of consciousness. This is not a delusion. It is not anything extraordinary either. Like awareness, sleep and dream state, this is a natural attribute of the entire mankind. It is easily accessible by all, may be with a little help initially. Even when not formally told about it, most of us are familiar with this altered state of consciousness. In ordinary experiences, childhood fairy tales, a beautiful landscape, a piece of fine poetry, an absorbing novel, a magnificent painting, or simply in a creative thought we catch glimpses of this natural attribute that all humans possess. A good glimpse of this not so unfamiliar dimension is obtained in mystic verses from various Eastern traditions. But the poets know not the boundaries of East and West. Therefore, William Blake sings about holding the infinity in the palm of one's hand and seeing eternity in an hour. Wordsworth describes his experience of the altered state of consciousness as:

For oft when on my couch I lie,
In vacant or in pensive mood.
They flash upon that inward eye
Which is the bliss of solitude,
And then my heart with pleasure fills
And dances with the daffodils.

And a nine-year-old daughter of a Nobel Laureate writes[6]:

If you ever get to infinity,
You will find me there;
For tomorrow I will climb
The elementary stair.
I will climb to the very top
Open up the door.
Look at all the ages
Lying on the floor.

Such intuitive connection remains only a glimpse for most of us, because, caught as we are in the cross traffic of the profit and loss in our worldly trade accounts, we are immediately drawn away from this almost 'other worldly' experience; only to remember it as some precious moments. The memory of the precious moments can and do turn into "ever present now". For this to happen, we have the doorway of the fourth state of consciousness.

The Fourth State of Awareness

All kind of meditative states begin with the Fourth State of consciousness. For the generation of the Fourth State of consciousness, most of the traditions rely on reflection, or self-absorption or simple relaxation along with deep breathing. There are sophisticated techniques for each of these but one need not be familiar with them to begin. As the process goes forward, within a few minutes there is spontaneous onset of the Fourth State of consciousness. Patanjali indeed calls it *turya;* that means the fourth state. The characteristics of this state are that the mind is quiet, calm and peaceful. A general sense of well-being prevails. The person is awake but the state is more like sleep than awake. It is a state of alert restfulness. In this state there is focalization on the subject of meditation, be it the image or the mantra and the marginal inputs fade. The focal point becomes symbolic, i.e. it gathers content that goes on expanding in its abstract meaning. There is attention on the focalized idea but it is not accompanied by any kind of tension. There may be distraction by the surroundings but there is no disturbance. There is choiceless extensive awareness but it is not exclusive of anything in particular.

The subjective time moves slowly and an hour may appear to have been only a few minutes. Or the time may so undulate that the distinction between the past, present and future is lost. There is shift of space location and one can experience oneself at several different locations in space during this state. This is trance. And in the state of trance, one may experience the space-time dimension to shift. It is possible to regress in time and be at places at times in the past, which may have been forgotten.

The state has been studied physiologically by Herbert Benson[7]. And there are extensive studies on the physiology of the Fourth State of consciousness induced through one of the methods of meditation-transcendental meditation technique[8, 9, 10]. Initially the pulse rate and the blood pressure rise; but soon go below the resting levels. The respiratory rate rises first but soon falls below the resting level and as the trance progresses, it may be accompanied by small periods of apnoea. The metabolic rate falls steeply and it may fall below the level of sleep. The peripheral flow of blood increases and the body and the face may be flushed. Plasma cortisol levels decline. There is increased coherence of functions of both the hemispheres of the brain. In the electroencephalogram there is preponderance of alpha waves. There is increase of the galvanic skin resistance.

For the regular practitioners of meditation, there are lasting psychological benefits. Overall the stress levels decline. There are better interpersonal relationships. There is realistic goal setting and achievement. There is overall increase in productivity and creativity. Probably the most important outcome of the meditative process is clarity of perception and the generation of intuitive insight.

This was stated to emphasize that the verifiable empirical data are available and the Fourth State is just not a philosophical speculation. But the greatest validation of the Fourth State is its subjective validation by most people in the very first attempt that they make to experience it. That is because, the experiential component, though subjective and appearing to be esoteric is the fundamental attribute of the mankind.

The highly aesthetic experience is given a poetical description by Aldous Huxley[11]. Huxley was drawn to Buddhism and had practiced meditation. His description of what happens in the Fourth State* is immaculate. Huxley states, "I was seeing what Adam had seen on the morning of his creation—the miracle, moment by moment, of naked existence." In an instant he experienced in things around him; a transience that was yet an eternal life, perpetual perishing, that was at the same moment, pure being. In this state, a simple look at the flower in the vase was to provide the beatific vision of *sat, chit, ananda,* viz. Being, Awareness and Bliss". He saw the *dharma* body of the Buddha in the flowers. The doors to a new way of perception seemed to be open. Spatial relationships ceased to matter. Instead there was intensity of existence, profundity of significance and relationships within a pattern. He instantaneously realized the experience of Van Gogh in the painting of the Chair. While Huxley gazed at the legs of the Chair, he experienced, "Being my Non-self in the Non-self that was the Chair."

---

* Huxley's description is following his personal experience with ingestion of muscaline. The meditation and the drug-induced state following muscaline are not identical. However, the description of the Fourth State is similar.

Alice's First Step into Wonderland

While meditation is easily accessible, a background state of simple understanding and righteous living is a prerequisite. Alice can easily step in Wonderland, but before that she has to realize that:

> There is truth of suffering, it arises and exists in accordance with twelve fold chain of causation[12]. This is made more explicit by saying it poetically thus:
>
> Due to the existence of this, that arises,
> Due to the production of this, that is engendered.
> It is thus: due to ignorance, there is volitional action;
> Due to action there is mind.

It is not easy to end suffering; even after understanding as to how it arises. For that one has to find a stable code for everyday living[13]. This is the basis of the Dalai Lama's recent book, Ethics for the New Millennium[10]. It is a prerequisite for the access to the gateway to the fourth state of consciousness. The reason is that the strife and turmoil of non-ethical life style produces so much stress and distraction that one cannot generate the alternative fourth state of consciousness, leave apart staying there for long. Therefore, the ethical conduct is specifically defined in Buddhism as well as by Patanjali.

One should avoid a sense of I-ness to the instrument of perception and action. Any sense organ, including the mind that we have already identified as an additional sense organ gives only an impression. Let it not be identified with self. In everyday living, one is led to several fallacies about perception. What is seen is colored by various projections of mind. What we discussed earlier as defenses of ego in terms of Freudian psychology, are indeed the diseases of mind that refuses to accept perceptual clarity. There is a constant striving by the mind to weigh each and every matter in its own favour. In the process, the concept of reality is tilted. The mind is a mirror that has a tendency to gather dust through stress and strife of everyday life. And this dust must not be allowed to remain. Better still the dust should not generate and if there is any, it must constantly be wiped out. J. Krishnamurty[14] has explained it thus:

How is a mind that has so many problems, to meet new problems? There is problem of time, the problem of space, the problem of relationship, and the problem of living, of earning a livelihood, the problem of disease, health and old age. How is the mind to meet all these problems all at once, not one by one but the whole of them all together, without effort? ... The way we meet them now, our problems are all fragmentary. There is the problem of fear, the problem of boredom, the problem of enjoyment—a multitude of problems one after the other. Is there a way of meeting all these problems not separately, but totally? ...For the mind to be totally free from pressure, pleasant or unpleasant, all motives, however subtle or noble, must wither away.

The experience of withering of all the motives cannot be given a name. But the protocol for experiencing the Nameless Experience is almost the same in Buddhism and Raj Yoga of Patanjali[15,16,17]. The preparation is by turning our mind to ethics, concentration and wisdom. An ethical code of living provides a substratum to the mind so that there is clear perception of the one's own motives leading to just action. This is a prelude to the stoppage of the dialectical wandering of the mind.

What happens to the mind following this path is a kind of transformation. It has been variously described as metamorphosis and mutation. There is awakening of intelligence[18] so that the very ground from where the intelligence arises undergoes a multifold transformation*.

This kind of the awareness is different from the ordinary awareness by which most people live. In this profound state of awareness, one is a participant and a witness too. Of course, on the way further, the participant and the witness both cease to be. Observer and observed also merge† to disappear altogether. The consciousness then assumes whatever form is presented to it, knower, known or the act of knowledge.

That is a state of self-realization. The intermediate steps differ somewhat between the Classical Indian mode and the Tibetan methods, but *samadhi*‡ and *sunyata* are the final destination in the timeless moment.

---

* *Tasya saptadha pranta-bhumi prajna*, Patanjali's Yoga Sutra Section II, 27.

† Patanjali's Yoga Sutra, Section III, 3.

‡ *Samadhi* is further categorized into *savikalpa* (with reflection) and *nirvikalpa* (non-reflective, completely void of all contents in the mind). Patanjali's Yoga Sutra, Section I; 42, 43.

In this state there is steadiness of perception without any object to hold on to and there is total stillness of mind without dependence on any image. It is this new mind that has come out of a radical transformation that can comprehend true nature of time.* There is a clear understanding that the perception of time is dependent on the moment of consciousness. While the past and future turn out to be mental constructs, the ever present *now* is just a moment, dependent on the consciousness[19]. Since consciousness itself is modulated in the meditative process, moment of *now* also subjects itself to change. Time dilation and constriction as well as stoppage of time are the natural outcome.

There is a whole section devoted to the development of special faculties of perception that are termed as *vibhuti* or *siddhi.*† The psychic powers become obvious at times without any effort so that one develops the faculty of knowing the mind of the other‡. One wonders how is it that Tibetan lamas, rimpoches, know about their previous birth. Patanjali says that by introspecting on ones inherent tendencies—*sanskara*—this is achieved. Phenomena like being in two places are the result of attainment on meditation on the body of the form and clairaudience comes about through meditation on sound.§ The *siddhi* of minutest perception, *anima,* comes about by further extension of faculties of vision. The meditator can then not only cognize the smallest particle but also perceive what is hidden or is at a distance¶. This would explain clairvoyance. The precise description of "occult chemistry" as well as "particle physics" of Jainism is said to be arrived at by meditating on solar system, moon and Polar star**.

Paranormal healing is said to arise by meditation on various *chakras* in the body. The *chakras* are said to be energy centers located in the body[20, 21]. Though they are abstract forms, their location corresponds with the plexuses of autonomic nervous systems.

---

* Patanjali's Yoga Sutra, Section III, 16.

† Patanjali's Yoga Sutra, Section III: 1-56.

‡ *Ibid.* Section III: 17, 19.

§ *Ibid.* Section III, 21, 22.

¶ *Ibid.* Section III, 26.

** The tantrik system relies heavily on deriving energy from the chakras as well as by the arousal of kundalini. The detailed description is out of place here but many of the miraculous physical feats of hatha yogis are ascribed to their mastery over this system.

The yoga has a highly intricate system of physiology. According to this system there are *chakras* and various *nadis* (very small nerves). *Muladhara chakra* is located at the base of the vertebral column at the root of the spinal cord. The other *chakras* in the ascending anatomical order are *svadhisthana, manipura, anahata and visuddha. Sahasrara* is located in the frontal region of the brain. A meditator can activate all these *chakras* and draw energy from them, and alternatively there is a process to arouse *kundalini*. While this is commonly described as "serpent power", its "anatomical" location is a nervous plexus at the termination of the spinal cord.

The *sidhdhis* accrue in the process of meditation. They are not to be pursued. The destination is *samadhi* or *kaivalya* where one is united with the One. It is a journey from alone to Alone. The individual consciousness transforms into universal consciousness. There are no qualities ascribed to such a state.

To the Eastern sensibilities, the meditative experience in varying degrees is elementary. It sounds all that esoteric to the West and the interest centers mainly on the physical and psychological attainment. Therefore some scientists, like Herbert Benson have wondered whether the effects produced by meditating on a *mantra* can also be brought about by silent recitation of nonsense, say 1,2,3; 1,2,3; 1,2,3 etc. They are entirely missing the point of symbolic visualization. A symbolic image has full content and can have portent meaning and so can the recitation of a particular *mantra*. It may be compared with a cultural archetype but it may have the power to be applicable to the entire mankind provided we carry out research into the lineages of languages. For instance there is a symbolic meaning of the *mantra, Om Mani Padme* Hum. Later we will see in Appendix III.

ENDNOTES

1. Collins James (1953). *The Mind of Kierkegaard,* Chicago.
2. Bhaskar Vyas and Rajni Vyas (2001). *The Collision of Culture,* New Delhi.
3. Rohit Mehta (1982). *Yoga: The Art of Integration, Commentaries on Yoga Sutras of Patanjali,* Adyar and London, pp. 233-373.
4. Taimni, I.K. (1961). *The Science of Yoga,* Adyar.
5. S. Radhakrishnan (1991). *Indian Philosophy,* Oxford, pp. 337-373.
6. George Wald (1983)., "Life and mind in the universe", In: *Evolution of Consciousness,* Ed. Kishore Gandhi, New Delhi.

7. Herbert Benson (1980), *The Relaxation Response*, Boston.
8. Maharshi Mahesh Yogi (1977). *Creating an Ideal Society*, Selisberg.
9. Wallace Robert Keith (1970). *The Physiological Effects of Transcendental Meditation: A Proposed Fourth Major State of Consciousness*, Los Angeles.
10. Orme, Johnson, D.W. and Farrow, J.T. (1976). *Scientific Research on the Transcendental Meditation Programme*, Collected papers, Meru, Switzerland.
11. Huxley, Aldous (1956). *The Doors of Perception*, London.
12. Suzuki, D.T. (1980). *Essays in Zen Buddhism*, First Series, London, p. 129.
13. The Dalai Lama (1999). *Ancient Wisdom, Modern World, Ethics for a New Millennium*, London.
14. Rohit Mehta (1979). *J. Krishnamurty and The Nameless Experience*, Delhi, pp. 128-153.
15. Warren, H.C. (1980). *Vishudhimagga*, London.
16. The Dalai Lama (1991). *Path to Bliss: A Practical Guide to Stages of Meditation*, New York, pp. 207-215.
17. Mehta Rohit (1990). *Yoga: The Art of Integration*, Madras, pp. 105-115.
18. J. Krishnamurty (1970). *Awakening of Intelligence*, Madras.
19. Dwarakanath Reddy (2003). *The Dicey Problem of New Age Science: Einstein, Hawking and God at the Casino*, Chittoor.
20. S. Radhakrishnan (1991). *Indian Philosophy*, Volume II, Oxford, p. 352.
21. C.W. Leadbeater (1927). *The Chakras*, Adyar, Madras.

6
Conclusion

Initially, the thesis aims at exploring the concepts of space, time and consciousness through the physical sciences as well as through the philosophical system of logical positivism. The limitations of scientific methodology as well as the philosophy of logical positivism become obvious, as both cannot explain paradoxes in physical sciences as well as empirical data in the form of paranormal occurrences.

Overview of the hitherto scattered scientific data about consciousness, lead us to a point where this epi-phenomenon in the matter may be "happening" at every point in a biological system where electric impulses are generated. That further translates that it may be an electromagnetic field. Quantum phenomena occur in physiological processes. The electromagnetic field then interacts with charged particles so as to bring about a quantum electro-dynamic field (QED). At the quantum level, space-time continuum becomes evident. If consciousness by itself is a QED field, it further combines with space-time continuum to bring about an additional dimension as space-time-consciousness. We call this the Fifth Dimension. Warping and field dragging of the space-time continuum then extends to the Fifth Dimension, so that undulation in the QED field of consciousness can trans-locate across past, present and future as well as all through the space, from here to eternity.

But the theory falls short of final touchstone of science. Where are the repeatable and reproducible experiments? Give us at least one equation, the physicists will say. We admit we do not have one so far. But then the scientists have no explanations for the paranormal either.

The Fifth Dimension is then explored through a paradigm

shift. Two Eastern worldviews, the Tibetan Buddhism and Raj Yoga of Patanjali are juxtaposed to the materialist worldview and are examined employing the philosophy of intuition.

We have reviewed the Modern Scientific Paradigm where the time dimension appears to move unidirectional forward at thermodynamic and electromagnetic level and, to an extent at psychological level. But the theories of physics leave us undecided with the precise knowledge about time and the violation of time invariance. At the cosmological level, the space-time co-ordinate tends to be curved instead of being a straight arrow of time. The nature of space is still to be further explored. The empty space is filled with immense energy. The consciousness for the materialist scientific mode is just a function of the brain and there is no independent existence apart from it. Therefore, there is no other self except the physical self.

The Buddhist Philosophical mode considers time as timeless. Its nature is cyclic, in terms of cyclic existence of consciousness that reincarnates. Space is all void but full of energy. The ultimate reality of the universe is this fullness of the void space filled with energy. All parameters of ultimate reality are covered under an over-riding paradigm of beginning-less consciousness.

The very nature of the coarse level of mind is changed to a subtle level through the medium of the Fourth State of Consciousness. Objective validation of the Fourth State of Consciousness is furnished. The glimpses of the Fifth Dimension through the route of the Fourth State of Consciousness are provided.

It is argued that if the consciousness is a field then there may be interaction with such other fields. Other fields may cause their effects in the way that known fields in the realm of physics do. Or consciousness may be a QED field around a subatomic particle-conscion, having no intrinsic rest mass. It may move at the speed of light if it has, like a photon a zero rest mass, then it shall be possible to explain its cosmic travel and such other states. Such a discovery will be a scientific transcendence—a quantum jump. Are these visions illusions? Are they only chimeras arising out of a deranged perception? Is the belief of the mankind only an archetypal hangover? Or, will such visualizations, that may be a perception of reality that is not perceived by the present day knowledge in material sciences, become a physical reality later on? Or, are they an echo of the nothingness?

The logical inconsistencies are in both the domains. However, there is a paradox of irrationality of the physical and rationality of the metaphysical. The physical sciences do not explain all; and if the sages do have the answers, they do not care to subject themselves to experimentation.

Table 6.1: Juxtaposing the Scientific Paradigm and Eastern Meditative way with Reference to Space-Time-Consciousness and Related Dimensions

Time	Thermodynamic and electromagnetic time a straight line, psychological time, questionable, cosmological time and time at the subatomic level under further exploration.	Timeless without a beginning and end, circular in the form of law of karmic connection, empirical data in the form of reincarnation studies.
Space	Empty, Capable of carrying fields like gravitation, and waves like light. Particles appear due to undulations produced by electric current. Empty space intensely surcharged with energy. Together with time, there is a fourth co-ordinate of space, space-time, which under the influence of gravitation, takes the nature of a curve, i.e. space-time becomes curvilinear.	Empty—sunyata. Intensely full of energy, phenomena arise according to a small undulation in the energy field.
Self	There is no other self except the physical self. Cartesian thinking of body and mind duality giving way to the concept of a single unity in body-mind. There is no existence of a mind separate from the body.	Buddhist view: there are three entities, body, coarse mind and subtle mind. Brain is only a cooperative cause for the subtle mind to exist. The subtle mind does not perish at the time of death but leaves the body either to higher realms, bardo and beyond. It either reincarnates or may go to Nirvana
Consciousness	It is the function of the specific areas of the brain. But no idea as to how does it arises. Vanishes as the specific part of the brain dies.	Consciousness is subtle mind. It never vanishes. It reincarnates. Or it merges with sunyata at nirvana. Classical Indian view: consciousness does not perish.

(Contd.)

Philosophical Postulate	Epistemological and empirical; Causality and change accepted as the basis of phenomena except at the level of quantum physics where randomness and chance are the rules.	Epistemological and empirical; no inherent existence of any phenomena; but the law of causality and change is immutable. Only by the cessation of all karmas can one go to nirvana.
Specific Feature	Falsifiability is the specific feature by which most advances in knowledge of phenomenology has advanced.	Envisages a fourth state of consciousness whereby one can generate the subtle mind that can transcend the ordinary dimensions of space and time. Experience of the Fifth Dimension is a natural attribute of the mankind through turya.
Paranormal Phenomena	Unexplained.	Explains reincarnation as well as anima and parapsychology.

That leaves us with Newton collecting pebbles on the seashore of knowledge and Einstein wondering at the play of dice: on the other hand, we are also confronted with the Buddha of Hinayana Buddhism. At the moment of enlightenment, Buddha is said to have thought, a Buddha alone is able to understand what the mind of another Buddha is. He sang thus:

> This that through many toils I've won,
> Enough! Why should I make it known?
> By folk with hate and lust consumed
> Not this Truth that can be grasped!
> Against the stream of common thought,
> Deep, subtle, difficult, delicate,
> Unseen 'twill be by passion slaves
> Cloaked in the murk of Ignorance.

The answer will come through a future Einstein who will discover "conscion" and by the future Vajrasattva Buddha and Patanjali who will teach the methods of experiencing and enhancing quantum electro-dynamic fields.

Appendices

Appendix I

Albert Einstein's reply to a Girl Child about Prayer

He wrote on 24 January 1936 as follows:

I have tried to respond to your question as simply as I could. Here is my answer:

Scientific research is based on the idea that the laws of nature determine everything that takes place and therefore this holds for the actions of people. For this reason a research scientist will hardly be inclined to believe that events could be influenced by a prayer, i.e. a wish that is addressed to a supernatural Being.

However, it must be admitted that our actual knowledge of these laws is only imperfect and fragmentary, so that, actually the belief in the existence of basic all embracing laws in Nature also rests on a sort of faith. All the same this faith has been largely justified so far by the successpage 82++ of scientific research. But on the other hand, everyone who is seriously involved in the pursuit of science becomes convinced that a spirit is manifest in the laws of the Universe—a spirit vastly superior to that of man, and one in the face of which we, with our modest powers, must feel humble. In this way the pursuit of science leads to a religious feeling of a special sort, which is indeed, quite different from the religiosity of someone more naïve.[11]

Appendix II

Freudian Concept of Ego Defenses

Freud and his daughter Anna, who also was a Freudian psychoanalyst, call certain attitudes of the mind as ego defenses. Such psychodynamics come into play when the sense of security is threatened and the resulting stress, when not taken into ones stride, calls for some prop up. This situation arises primarily because Freud conceptualizes ego in the state of a delicate balance that is constantly threatened. Since we do not agree with the construct of Freudian depth psychology, there cannot be any agreement in terms such as defenses of the ego. However, the so-called defenses are commonplace occurrences in psychologically ill people seen in everyday life. These machinations of mind add color to the perception and distort the reality.

Freud believes that whenever ego is threatened in its efforts to maintain a balance between the conflicting demands of id and restrictive impositions of super-ego, it brings into operation a series of highly structured modifications in perception. They serve as means for viewing the situation differently. Such defenses can be narcissistic like *projection* of one's impulses onto someone else or outside of one's self; thus neurotic projection would entail perceiving and reacting to unacceptable inner impulses and their derivatives as though they were outside of one's self. *Denial* entails refusal of the actual external reality. *Repression and denial* affect the external reality more than inner reality. So much so that a person may have nothing wrong with eyesight, but would refuse to acknowledge what is seen: similarly ears may be normal but the person may refuse to acknowledge what is heard. A person may grossly redefine the external reality to suit the inner needs through a trait termed as *distortion*. Distortion takes the form of grossly reshaping external reality to satisfy one's personal needs such as sustained feelings of superiority or megalomaniac beliefs. This is seen particularly amongst politicians and in the people who play politics in whatsoever field that they belong.

Freud describes another category of defenses as immature defenses by the ego. The immature neurotic defenses are easy to detect. Their operation involves *acting out* which is a direct expression of an unconscious impulse or wish; *blocking*, whereby there is inhibition of affect and thinking; *hypochondriasis*, where there are imaginary symptoms of illness which in reality does not exist. This can progress to *somatization* whereby there are real illnesses. *Introjections* are much more complex. This involves internalization of the traits of an object of love into one's own personality that causes a shift of matrix of relationships. Introjections and *externalization* involve the tendency to perceive in the external world one's own personality. All such vagaries of mind may then produce *regression* to an earlier phase of psychological development.

A further step in distorted perception by the mind, termed as *neurotic defenses* include *displacement* that is brought about by purposeful shifting from one object to other. Displacement is a useful defense of the ego and frequently employed as a purposeful though unconscious shifting from one object or activity of interest to another in the interest of solving a conflict. A temporary but drastic modification of personal identity to avoid emotional distress occurs by the way of *dissociation*. Neurosis can express in other diverse forms such as *internalization*, which is reverse attitude to externalization mentioned above.

The progression leads us to *intellectualization* whereby there is too much of thinking involved about one's own affects and impulses rather than just experiencing them. *Intellectualization* and *rationalization* are contrived efforts by the psyche to account for/justify the attitudes that are otherwise not acceptable and by this mental exercise, to control the affect and impulses instead of experiencing them. Rationalization frequently afflicts scientists—even Einstein was not an exception* and the mystic alike and involves justification of attitudes, beliefs or behaviour that might otherwise be unacceptable. The apparently logical arguments are advanced by application of unjust reasons or there may be invention of a convincing *fallacy*. The list further includes *inhibition, isolation, reaction formation* and true to Freudian context, *sexualization*. *Repression* is one of the very important neurotic defenses. Here the unpleasant events are repressed into deeper layers of subconscious or unconscious mind. However, it cannot be missed that from there,

* Recall the famous quote, "God cannot be playing dice!"

they are bound to exercise compelling influences that modulate behaviour and cause illness.

Freud enlarged the concept of ego to include even *altruism, asceticism and sublimation* as one kind of mind modulation in the defense of self! No doubt then, that such a concept of self was without any inherent sense of virtue. It did not have any roots in any kind of values.

Appendix III

Some Illustrative Tibetan Buddhist Meditative Practices

Meditation on Metta, Compassion

The well-charted path begins from the common ground that pertains to all of us. The recommended first step is to meditate on metta[2], i.e. compassion. The beginner is advised to appreciate how much his life depends on the kindness of others. Even then compassion may not arise of its own. This universal love is not the customary/habitual attitude of the mind. It must be cultivated. The cultivation is easy to begin firstly with oneself. A person finds no difficulty to reflect upon how one's own well being has to be looked after. It should then follow that the others also have the same desires and are equally entitled to happiness.

Meditation on metta is aimed at the liberation of the mind from hatred, ill-will, anger and selfishness. In the beginning the meditator affirms his self-love, viz. that is his own concern for freedom from the enmity. It soon leads to the understanding that the others also have the same concern for their own well-being. So it is natural to wish them their welfare and happiness. Then he extends his love to those who are his family members and friends; then to the neutral people and then even to those who are his enemies or for whom he has hostile feelings.

When the aversion is experienced, one reflects on the law of cause and effect, or the *karmic* connection. There may have been such connection in the past that the enemy is hostile to him. It may be possible to know or it is lost in the past. But the *karmic* connection is operative all the time. An act of aversion, hostility or enmity now to the hated person would bring out harm in two ways—it will breed further enmity and, even before that the negative feelings will do self-damage.

The Dalai Lama's advice[3] is to begin by reflecting on the selfless love of a mother. Imagine the motherhood prevalent in all beings in nature and take it further to the thought that all of them could be your mothers. But such altruistic activities, though admired by the most, may not be practicable by all. The Tibetan Buddhist practices have a recipe of the most varied variety. It is said that there are at least a few thousand methods to practice meditation and one can choose to suit one's own disposition. For those who are inclined to be rational and analytical, *vipassyana* is a good method to begin.

Samata Meditation

There are other methods, and a teacher may facilitate the choice after knowing one's disposition. Torn as we are in the modern civilization by the pulls of opposites, another common offering is *samata* meditation. This teaches equipoise and is again based on the standard precepts of dependent origination that guides to the ultimate realization of *sunyata*.

Single Pointed Mind

These methods are suitable for beginners. It requires quite some preparation initially to follow the ethical life but two can proceed simultaneously. Such a practice would certainly make us better human beings. But if the glimpse of the Fifth Dimension is the aim, it is still too far. Having begun to meditate, the experience of the Fourth State of consciousness is enough of an incentive to enhance aspiration.[*],[†]

From this state of reflective meditation, that will have cultivated the coarse mind, one has then to progress to a single pointed method so as to have a direct intuitive experience of *sunyata*. As soon as we understand the nature of *sunyata* even at the cognitive level; the first step is made. And such a practice does generate an aspiration for bodhichitta[4]—a compassionate wish to attain Buddhahood for the benefit of others. This knowledge is the path of connection to

---

* Sri Aurobindo described the Fourth State of consciousness as the realm of overmind. In this state, the most distinctive features are cessation of discursive, dialectic mental process and experience of peace that is unique. He therefore called it a corridor between mind and supermind. To confirm to the terminology of Tibetan tradition, we may call it a corridor between the coarse mind and subtle mind to very subtle mind.

† There is great correspondence between the Tibetan tradition and Indian tradition of Patanjali. But to avoid confusion in terms and better comparison the Indian tradition is laid out in Appendix V.

the higher realms. Now the meditative practice will lead us to the higher *yoga tantra* where the intuitive realization of emptiness is experienced.

Vipassyana Meditation

Vipassyana meditation begins by reflection on the body; first it aims at observing the breath. In a placid state, one sits quietly and observes the coming and going of the breath. It gently spreads over the body in the form of observation of the body and ponders over its nature. This is *kayanupassana*: that is observation of the body. Here the flow of the breath and the memory of the body are the objects of contemplation. The next step is to observe one's feelings in the form of *vedana-anupassana*, where the flow of feelings is meditated upon. This generates insight. The contents of the mind are reflected on and then the process is called *chitta-anupassana*. Reflection on the philosophical aspects of religious experience, Nature, inherent quality, void, merit and *samadhi* is *dhammanupassana*. It is the final stage of *vipassana* meditation.

Vajrayana Practice

The practices we discussed so far belong to Mahayana tradition. They are helpful in eliminating the agitation of the coarse mind. One can be a guide to one's own path so far. The Vajrayana practices* are very sophisticated and profound in meaning[5, 6, 7, 8, 9]. The core of the method is to focus single pointedly at one or more images. The image can be a pebble, a piece of wood or any other object on your study table[10]. It could preferably be an image of a deity—may be Christ or any other symbolic image according to one's belief. But this should not be equated with image worship. The images of the deities are symbolic in content; say *avalokiteshwar* Buddha connotes the virtue of compassion, *amitabh* Buddha connotes the merit of wisdom, or for that matter Tara symbolizes the energy and might. Either a single image may be preferred or there may be many as per the method. Instead of, or in addition to, there can be a silent recitation of a *mantra*, say *Om Mani Padme Hum.*

---

* A guru or a guide if one may like to call is needed. Even an initiation, meaning empowerment is mandatory.

Om Mani Padme Hum[11]

There are several *mantras*, but this one is said to be a root *mantra*. Om is composed of three letters, A, U, and M. They symbolize the pure exalted body, speech and mind of a Buddha. The development of pure body, speech, and mind comes from gradually leaving the impure state. The path is indicated by *Mani* meaning the jewel. It symbolizes the altruistic intention to become enlightened through compassion and love. The selfless mind of enlightenment is capable of removing the poverty or difficulty of cyclic existence. The word, *Padme*, meaning lotus, symbolizes the wisdom. Through wisdom, one arrives at the situation of non-contradiction. Impermanence is realized. There is wisdom that realizes (i) that the persons are empty of being substantially existent and (ii) the emptiness of duality so that it brings about the awareness of the emptiness of inherent existence.

Purity must be achieved by an indivisible unity of method and wisdom, symbolized by the final word, *hum*. In the *mantra* it refers to one consciousness in which there is full form of both, wisdom and method. So that the two cannot be differentiated and they become a single entity. *Hum* is the seed syllable of *Akshobhya*— immovable, the non-fluctuating, that which cannot be disturbed by anything.

Kalachakra* Initiation

Kalachakra meditation is the highest form of Vajrayana initiation.

In the entire Tibetan tradition the Dalai Lama and only a few others are entitled to give this initiation. Initiation is like the empowerment ceremony—the inauguration of an elected person to an office. He has to be worthy of it by first acquiring merit and when thought suitable, he/she is given initiation. The ceremony lasts for about a week. An elaborate *mandala* is prepared with the symbolic deities located inside. *Kalachakra mandala* has 928 images to meditate upon in rapid succession, imbibing the virtue of each symbol within oneself in the process of meditation.

The essence of the Vajrayana path is that it combines method and wisdom in the most impeccable way. This is so because a virtue or merit is initially attributed to the symbol, that is internalized

* For details please refer to refs. 4, 5, 6, 7, 8.

and at the end of the meditation, dissolved into the all pervading emptiness. This is generative of the subtle mind that gives the glimpse of the Fifth Dimension. There are several other methods but particularly relevant to our discussion on consciousness, is the method called *po-wa* visualizations in preparation for death. It incorporates the *kundalini** yoga too.

Preparation for Death: po-wa Visualization

A practitioner may say to himself thus[12]:

I have received teachings on the principal paths. I have meditated on them. I have received Vajrayana instructions and tried to practice them faithfully. But I have discovered that it is not possible for me to attain enlightenment in this life...so I intend to practice *po-wa* (literally translates as, transference of consciousness) to Amitabh's pure land. When the time of death comes, one transfers very subtle energy together with very subtle mind to the central channel of the spinal cord up to the crown of the head and out from there into Amitabh's pure land.

The exact steps of the practice are to visualize the central channel that should be seen as closer to the back, a little bit in front of spine. The channel is closed at the bottom but open at the crown of the head. Then the fundamental energy of the seed-syllable, i.e. *tig-le* is seen sitting like a small pea within the central channel at the level of the heart. Then make attempt to move the seed-syllable up and down the central channel. The seed syllable is brought to the level of the crown where the central channel is open. From the vantage point of the opening of the central channel, an attempt is made to look inside the channel. Go up and down the channel and see you cleaning up its interior.

Now visualize Amitabh Buddha seated in space in front of you at the level of the forehead. He is ruby red in color and his entire body is made out of transparent radiant light. See yourself

---

* *Kundalini* yoga aims at awakening the root source of energy. It has anatomical basis. Initially there is focalization at the root of the spinal cord, on the sacral plexus. Energy is visualized lying coiled up over there. It is nudged to 'wake up', where after it ascends along the nervous plexuses on both the sides of spinal cord, into what is described as *chakras,* way up to the forebrain into the *Sahasrara chakra.*

take refuge in the Amitabha and then see the radiant light energy coming from him down into the central channel. See it purifying you completely of all the hindrances. By means of such purification see the body slowly transform from gross physical to that of radiant light.

Now see the seed-syllable transforming itself. It is white in color, clear as crystal with a slight reddish tint. It has become now a small radiant point of light, tiny vibrating star. Move it up and down the channel. Clean up all the *chakras* as it moves up and down the channel.

Breathe in deeply and at the same time tighten the lower muscles slightly at the level of the bottom of the body. Thus, when the energy from the intake of your breath meets the tightened up energy from your bottom muscles, it makes you experience a blissful feeling. When you have done this for a few times and your blissful state has intensified, let go of the feeling all-together. It gives you a practice to give up something intensely pleasurable.

Now visualize the channel in front of you. Choose a dimension that is convenient. But it is seen open at the top like a lotus flower. And when you go to sleep tonight, see yourself going to the pure land of Amitabh through the opening at the top. Having learnt this technique, it will be possible to let go your subtle, very subtle level of mind out of the open central channel and take rebirth according to your wish.

Where does such meditative practice lead us? Without reinforcing the concept of the subtle mind, it is not easy to see the inherently non-existent, ever changing from moment to moment, only a conceptually designated, mere self[13]. It has the functions as the other physical implements do. But that is not the real self. The real self is the subtle mind, the consciousness that is without a beginning and without an end. The dissolution in *nirvana* is there, but it is neither the beginning nor the end. If the non-reality of the conceptual mere self is realized, then only one will be able to appreciate that even though, the essence of life, i.e. *tig-le* is said to be located in the heart, in a heart transplanted person it makes no difference when he performs *po-wa* meditation.

Caution!

A word of caution about Vajrayana practice is needed[14]. These are highly technical mental "exercises", to put it very mildly. They cannot be undertaken without full preparation, initiation and supervision. Sometimes most extraordinary symptoms do appear. The following case report will illustrate the point.

An overzealous young *karate* student decided to meditate and not move a full day and night. When he got up, he was filled with explosive energy. He strode into the middle of the dining hall filled with 100 silent retreating participants and began to yell and practice his *karate* maneuvers at triple speed...Then he made statements like, "when I look at each of you I see behind you a whole trail of bodies showing your past lives".

Appendix IV

Meditative Steps as per the Classical Indian Tradition of Patanjali

Patanjali's meditative way envisages Eight Steps*. To begin with, akin to the Tibetan tradition, he lays great stress on the ethical conduct in everyday living and has enunciated a moral code of do's and don'ts. But there after there is quite some divergence in the method. All the same, both lead to the Fourth State of consciousness.

There is much emphasis on posture and deep breathing of a particular type. The next step is *pratyahar,* an act of withdrawal. It is the meeting point of outer and inner disciplines. It is the process of rendering one's consciousness as free from sensorial inputs as possible. This is achieved by ignoring the inputs from the surroundings as well as the sixth sense organ, i.e. mind. It is the process of passive alertness where the senses, brain and mind are put to a state of restful awareness. It may be termed overmind consciousness that is a corridor. This leads to a shift of the paradigm. It is then followed by *dharana.*

In the stage of *dharana,* there is taking of a *mantra* or holding to an image that suits the sensibilities of the individual. This becomes the focal point of all levels of mind and all other inputs become marginal so that they gradually fade away from awareness. This leads to a single pointed concentration—*dhyana.*

In the state of *dhyana,* the totality of attention is directed upon the object that is being meditated till such time that there is dissolution of the image or fading away of the *mantra.* This leads to a state of *samadhi.* It is difficult to describe but the nearest description is that there is total cessation of thought and there is a vast expansion of consciousness so that all the paranormal phenomena may occur naturally and spontaneously. In other words, what is paranormal

---

* The Eight Steps are various modes of abstinence, certain observance, posture, breath-control, abstraction-detachment from the sensorial input, awareness, attention and communion. Patanjali's Yoga Sutra, Section II, 29.

in our four dimensional universe becomes a normal occurrence with the paradigm shift to the Fifth Dimension.

The paranormal occurrences are of eight types. Each one of them is termed as *vibhuti*[15,16,17] or *siddhi*. They are in the form of transcendence over the space and time. They are, *mahima, laghima, garima, prapti, prakamya, ishita, vashita,* i.e. making oneself very large, very light, very heavy, have capacity to reach any where, having all desires fulfilled, having the power to create and power to bring anything under one's control. These kinds of faculties come into operation of their own. They are purely incidental and need not be cultivated. It is described as the opening of the third eye. For achieving this, the state of *samadhi*—transcendence to Fifth Dimension—is a must.

The Classical Indian concept is that of one single universal consciousness. Individual experience as unitary, singular, self-confined consciousness is arbitrary. In the state of *samadhi* there is communion of individual experience with universal consciousness. This is described as compassion, love, *satori* and *sunyata*. Patanjali calls the state as *kaivalya,* where the consciousness is just that Alone.

Endnotes

Appendices I-IV

1. Albert Einstein (1979). *The Human Side,* Princeton University Press, Princeton.
2. Ratanakul P. (1991). *The Buddhist Ethics of Metta,* Paper given at the Sion Conference on Ethical Reflections, Netherlands, October 1991.
3. The Dalai Lama (1997). *The Four Noble Truths,* New Delhi, pp. 120-121.
4. The Dalai Lama (2000). The Way to Freedom. Core Teachings of Tibetan Buddhism, Dharmashala, 2000, p. 133.
5. Anil Kumar Sarkar (1993). *The Mysteries of Vajrayana Buddhism from Atisha to Dalai Lama,* New Delhi, pp. 157-173, 205.
6. Geshe Kelsang Gyatso (1997). *Essence of Vajrayana: The Highest Yoga Tantra Practice of Heruka Body Mandala,* London. pp. x-xii.
7. Geshe Nyawang Dhargyey (1985). *Kalachakara Tantra,* Dharmashala, 1985.

8. Geshe, Lhumdub Sopa, Jackson, R. and Newman, J. (1991). *The Wheel of Time: The Kalachakra in Context*, New York.
9. John Blofeld (1970). *The Way of Power, A Practical Guide to the Tantric Mysticism of Tibet*, London, pp. 190-218.
10. The Dalai Lama (1991). *Path to Bliss: A Practical Guide to Stages of Meditation*, New York, p. 194.
11. The Dalai Lama (1985). *Kindness, Clarity, and Insight*, Ed. Jeffrey Hopkins and Elizabeth Napper, pp. 116-117.
12. Lama Thumten Yeshe (1991), *Transference of Consciousness at the Time of Death*, Boston, pp. 1-42.
13. Hayward, J.W. and Franscisco Varela (1992). *Gentle Bridges, Conversation with the Dalai Lama on the Science of Mind*, Boston, pp. 106-125.
14. Walsh and Roche (1979). "Caution", *Am. J. Psychiatry* 136; 1085.
15. Collins James (1953). The Mind & Kierkegaard, Chicago.
16. Bhaskar Vyas and Rajni Vyas (2001). *The Collision of Culture*, New Delhi.
17. Rohit Mehta (1982). *The Art of Integration, Commentaries on Yoga Sutras of Patanjali*, Adyar and London, pp. 233-373.

Index